Mo

Encounters and Journeys

Jane Coates

Unless indicated otherwise, Scripture quotations are taken from the Holy Bible,
New International Version, NIV, or
The Message, MSG
New Living Translation, NLT
The Amplified Bible, AMP
King James Version, KJV
Good News Translation, GNT
The Living Bible, TLV

ISBN: 978-1-0369-2737-0

Printed and bound in Great Britain by T&P Print Ltd

Contents

Introduction

Jane's husband, Phil writes: This second book by Jane Coates was finished on 28 April 2025 – the day Jane died, following a year of what she regularly called 'her journey', after being diagnosed with an aggressive breast cancer in April 2024. She insisted on the final article (on The C Journey – see later) being sent to the pastoral care team from her room in the Bexley Wing, St James's Hospital, Leeds during the morning; she died later that evening. I had shown Jane the contents of the book on computer screen at home a few days earlier, and she had chosen the picture for the cover of this second book.

The Introduction to the first book, "Encounters and Journeys" is included here as it well describes the background to the articles comprising the various chapters – even though it refers specifically to chapters in the first book, I have left this unchanged both for simplicity and because it reflects Jane's personal and grounded spiritual expression of a living faith. My apologies for this repetition to the many who have read and valued Jane's first book – but maybe it will bring yet more to also read the first book. That book has gone around the world, to many in the Far East, Australasia, Europe and North America – many people who knew us, so it finds a ready place in their hearts, or people to whom it has been passed to by a friend or relative. The significant feedback is how helpful, valuable and treasured this book has been to readers around the world – a life beyond our original expectations, in God's gracious hands, ministering to many, pointing to Jesus.

Jane's introduction to her first book, "Encounters and Journeys"
(March 2023)
When the Covid Pandemic occurred and the first Covid Lockdown happened in April 2020, most of us found ourselves at home each day and every day, which was a new and challenging experience for us all. School children, students and University students were required to be at home, and working from home, home schooling, and study became the new norm. This was particularly challenging for parents who were able to go to their place of work or office and yet had the responsibility and care of home schooling their school aged children, and college students. It was a time of change, and challenge, and many readjustments were needed.

Families with children needed to find new ways to be family together, especially as in the first 'lockdown' only one hour per day of outside physical activity was prescribed and permitted. My husband, my grandson, Sam, and I had to develop a new daily routine of activity, work, recreation, and on-line lessons, with a cycle ride every day, board games and social activities each evening and discovering the joys of baking- along with just about everyone else. So, any excess weight that we lost with cycling was soon added back on again with the calories gained from eating the numerous cakes, muffins, scones, biscuits, and puddings. We all discovered and developed new skills and activities. It was a difficult journey for all of us.

During the three Covid Lockdown periods, I wrote letters and cards to friends, church members and contacts, to keep in touch, to support them from a distance, and to help them to feel that they were not so isolated. At the beginning of April 2020, coinciding with the first Lockdown, I started to write a Monday morning devotional email called Monday Thoughts and Prayers for the Pastoral Care Team that was connected to my church. I was the Pastoral Care Coordinator, with a Team of twelve Pastoral Carers, who each supported friends and members in the church. During the Lockdown periods we supported over eighty elderly and vulnerable members of the congregation with regular phone calls, emails, walks, garden visits and gifts, in addition to those people who were supported by our Seniors Worker and the Lunch Club members. The weekly Monday Thoughts and Prayers was a way of keeping the team connected, and supported, and was intended to be an encouragement to the team at such a difficult time in addition to sharing matters of concern for prayer. Every Monday morning, I would send out the email, as meeting face to face was almost impossible. It is hard to imagine that my Monday devotional messages and reflections have continued for three years. They continue to be well received by many people and not just by the original Pastoral Care Team as was the intention in the beginning. As other people began to hear about the Monday Thoughts or had received forwarded copies from friends, then the circulation list grew and become far wider. Many of the devotionals made their way on to the church's website.

When my small writing venture began, the devotionals were needed for connection and the encouragement of a group of people at a very difficult time. I had never written in this way before. I am not a trained Bible teacher or scholar, although I studied Theology for a two-year period as part of my university degree. But I have been on my personal journey with Christ from being a teenager, and so I have been able to speak and reflect from my personal, Christian, family, church experience and life experience in general.

I believe that the Holy Spirit gives a nudge, a prompt, or in my words a bit of a 'niggle' in the back of the mind that just won't go away, when He wants to initiate something new. My writing began in just that way- with a gentle push. I never imagined that I could be a writer. But often, I would wake in the night with just a single word or a phrase that would be the heart of a new Monday Thought. In the strange times that we experienced because of Covid, it seemed that God was perhaps doing new things in surprisingly new and different ways with each of us, and that He wanted to use each person in perhaps an unexpected way. God has a purpose for each one of us-and that 'new' thing may be something different and surprising that you or I could not have anticipated. That new thing may be a fresh encounter or an exciting new journey with God.

My three years' worth of weekly devotionals have been gathered and presented in book form for a wider audience. The devotionals are here presented in separate chapters under the title of Encounters and Journeys. The series called Encounters, explores how Jesus encountered different individuals in the Gospel accounts. In each of these episodes and narratives, I have attempted to step into the life and mind of the individual and to write from their perspective- what they might have thought, felt, or experienced. I imagined that I was the person that Jesus was meeting, or the bystander, and so I wrote the account in the first person. This experience was a little like 'hot seating', a technique that I had often used with school children to help them to understand the character in a story. This way of 'stepping into the story or the account,' or 'getting between the pages' helped me to appreciate more the perspective and experience of the character of each person that Jesus encountered, and to see in a deeper way how Jesus responded to each one.

The series called Lessons in the Desert, is based on Bible accounts of groups or individuals who had the hard experience of wandering or being in a desert place. The desert can be a harsh place, but it can also be a very beautiful place. Abram, Moses, Elijah, David, Jonah, John the Baptist and of course Jesus, all experienced desert life, experiences, and times, and had their own journeys in the desert.

Many of the early devotionals were personal experiences from family and personal life but reflections linked with Bible passages. These Monday Thoughts followed experiences such as a dislocated shoulder, a memory jar, a piece of knitting, sunflowers, the baobab tree, the need for oil, roots, a song, and a range of other unconnected things. A random collection of thoughts to dip in and out of.

I loved writing 'thoughts' about real objects, such as a dry-stone wall, a cushion, a lump of clay, a walking stick or a set of oars and drawing out some key lessons from them. We had recently moved to a converted old barn and looking out of my window I could see an ancient, imperfect, dry-stone wall. I loved the imagery of the old wall with its odd, shaped stones placed and built together by a master builder to form a wonderful structure. It spoke to me of God the master builder, Jesus the chief cornerstone, and the church with its living stones-people of different identities, cultures, backgrounds, shapes, and sizes. Imperfect people, with rough edges, that sometimes rubbed against each other, but each one needed and carefully placed.

Some sections of the book have connected thoughts and themes following a series. The Beatitudes of Jesus- or the beautiful attitudes; the names of God, Songs of Significance, Advent, Christmas, Easter, and my key words of life.

This is a book that is not intended to be read from the beginning to the end in any formal way. I hope that you will read sections and pages in any order that you choose. In this book, Encounters and Journeys, I hope that it will help you to encounter Jesus in new and fresh ways and that your journey with Him will take you to new places that perhaps were never on your itinerary. I trust that you will be blessed and encouraged by these pages.

Jane Coates

Introduction to this book:
More Encounters and Journeys

The Introduction to this second book is based on my conversations with Jane as we put the book together, with input from Laura, John and Sam. This second book brings together, in themes, the articles shared each week as 'Monday Thoughts and Prayers' by email, and on the Moortown Baptist Church website, from April 2023 to April 2025.

Jane has again written from her heart, to share truths, encourage and help the reader to follow Jesus in a daily walk, in Jane's rooted, grounded, compassionate way. She again draws much on her (and our) personal experience and life lessons from objects around us. We are aware that these speak to our everyday walk, and encourage us to go onwards.

Jane wished to include again her series called Encounters, which she previously noted "*explores how Jesus encountered different individuals in the Gospel accounts. In each of these episodes and narratives, I have attempted to step into the life and mind of the individual and to write from their perspective- what they might have thought, felt, or experienced. I imagined that I was the person that Jesus was meeting, or the bystander, and so I wrote the account in the first person. This experience was a little like 'hot seating', a technique that I had often used with school children to help them to understand the character in a story. This way of 'stepping into the story or the account,' or 'getting between the pages' helped me to appreciate more the perspective and experience of the character of each person that Jesus encountered, and to see in a deeper way how Jesus responded to each one.*" This chapter is included again at Jane's wish, as it expresses the heart of Jesus, and Jane's sense of this heart of love: Jesus said, "I am gentle and lowly in heart". The chapters on Jesus, and the I AM's further point directly to Jesus.

The chapter, The C Journey, is particularly poignant to us, as it will be to many, as it represents Jane's writing of her own journey – a difficult one in the year from April 2024, as I witnessed, but one where her faith in the goodness of God remained strong, as she continued to follow Jesus, giving herself to others, even when so unwell herself and finding so many difficulties in daily life to be overcome.

The Wilderness chapter reflects further the common life Lessons from the Desert in book 1. Similarly, a holiday in New York strongly stimulated 'object lesson' thoughts for Jane.

Jane was keen to include Esther, albeit briefly, to coincide with the Jewish celebration of Purim, and reflecting how a brave woman was able to make a historic difference for a whole nation. The stories of the many significant (not necessarily significant in their position in society) women in scripture teaches us how greatly God values women and men. I believe that Jane had a real heart for women and children, not least those who are most at risk in our society, as expressed in her professional life and her whole demeanour.

Joshua is significant to Jane and myself – at our wedding reception we sought to reflect in our words our determination – together - to follow Joshua's heart for God – "as for me and my house, we will serve the Lord". This is a great inspirational statement when you are young and bold – but demanding! It is one we have found, as time goes by, to be a basis of our lives – not just to worship but to serve our Lord, in daily ways (despite many failings en route). However, mercifully the New Testament makes very clear that this is not through our own abilities, but through Christ, and with a gracious Father who knows we are like 'jars of clay', yet containing the greatest treasure, the knowledge of Jesus and his presence in our hearts. The third person-related chapter is on Mother Theresa. Jane worked as a volunteer with the Baptist Missionary Society in Kolkutta, helping street children linked with Mother Theresa's ministry there, and was much affected by this, having herself been so involved professionally with the prevention of cruelty to children, and the wellbeing of children – a major flavour in Jane's life.

Advent captures one of the most significant seasons for Christians, despite the forces of commercialisation. The book ends with some Prayers – Jane loved the early Christian prayers and included some here to lift us up.

Jane noted for book 1 sentiments that fully apply to book 2, so she should have the last word: *"This is a book that is not intended to be read from the beginning to the end in any formal way. I hope that you will read sections and pages in any order that you choose. In this book, Encounters and Journeys, I hope that it will help you to encounter Jesus in new and fresh ways and that your journey with Him will take you to new places that perhaps were never on your itinerary. I trust that you will be blessed and encouraged by these pages."*

Phil Coates, June 2025
Jane Coates, 1950 – 2025

Jane Coates - a Lifetime of Adventures

Jane Coates was married to Phil for almost fifty-four years and they have four adult children and seven grandchildren. They have always lived in Leeds which is their hometown also.

Jane was born at home in Beeston, Leeds to Margaret Iris McNab and Robert "Sandy" McNab who already had a boy, Robert Stuart. Sandy was from the McNab clan of Scotland and Jane inherited the strength and fortitude to be expected of someone half Scots (Glaswegian) and half Yorkshire. She had a happy childhood. She attended Cross Flatts Primary School, then Thoresby Girls High School in central Leeds. A significant feature of her teenage years was her group of friends at school; they formed a key part of a youth group at Hunslet Baptist Church.

Jane's encounter with Jesus began when she was a teenager. She became a Christian age 16 going forward at a Billy Graham crusade streamed to Leeds in 1966, and was baptised at Hunslet Baptist Church in 1967. Phil came to this church in early 1967 and they began 'courting' in December 1967 when Jane was17 and Phil 19. They became engaged and got married on 3 July 1971, just after Jane finished her degree final exams. Jane was 21 on honeymoon.

They were much involved in evangelism, including Beach Missions around the UK, and started children's work in south Leeds. From the beginning of their relationship they were a duo singing gospel folk songs to support an extensive range of evangelistic meetings around the country, from small coffee bars to a packed Leeds Town Hall - even singing for a beach mission on their honeymoon in Llandudno (together with a surprise visit from Jane's parents)!

Their first home was in Rothwell, Leeds. They were heavily involved in Hunslet, running together - a key word - open air children's meetings, Bible clubs, plus Jane teaching Sunday School.

Jane was the first in her family to go to University. She obtained a degree in Psychology (with Theology) in 1971 and subsequently 3 postgraduate qualifications. The first part of her professional career was in social work. After a year working as a generic social worker in Leeds, she obtained the social work qualification (CQSW) with an additional qualification in Psychiatric Social Work (Cert PSW) from Leeds University in 1973. She worked as a Child Protection Worker for the NSPCC (1973-75), the Family Therapy Team at St. James's University Hospital, Leeds (1975-6) and with the NSPCC again (1982-4).

Jane and Phil's first two children, Emma and Charlotte were born in 1975 and 1977. Around 1980 they moved across the city for schools for the children, and began attending Moortown Baptist Church. Jane was much involved in mother and children groups, Sunday School teaching and linking people. She was aware from her own circumstances of the potential for isolation of mothers with young children and so was committed to running or helping run parent and children groups, and to Sunday School teaching all of her church life. These groups were crucial in touching the community outside the church and welcoming them in. She hosted and co-led a housegroup with Phil, which nurtured many people central to our church and the wider world mission.

Jane had always wanted a big family but had 3 early miscarriages in the 7 years after Charlotte was born. But in 1984 Laura was born, then John in 1986. It was difficult to continue a career in social work with four young children in the family, so Jane spent a year *retraining* to be a primary school teacher after having Laura and John, a further example of giving herself to the family whilst also having the career she worked so hard for. She completed a P.G.C.E. Primary in 1990 (Leeds Metropolitan University) and was a primary school teacher in Leeds for the next 27 years, teaching in several tough inner City Schools, (which was social work plus teaching really).

Most of Jane's teaching was with challenging children, many of whom had behavioural, social, family, and emotional difficulties, in addition to learning difficulties, and many with English as an additional language (EAL). She had Leadership and Senior Management responsibilities at her last school, a challenging inner-city school, for six and a half years as: the science coordinator (with a ground-breaking after school science club); religious education and collective worship coordinator; team leader for performance management; leader of the environment science team developing the new school grounds; - *and* full time year 2 class teacher! In 1999 she was a finalist in the TES/Pfizer Primary Teacher of Science; but she never did anything for an award or glory. She later taught as a supply teacher for some years, to give her flexibility for overseas volunteering.

Jane was awarded a Teacher Sabbatical in 2003 which consisted of 3 elements. The first was a visit to Bangladesh in February 2003, with the Baptist Missionary Society (BMS). This very formative volunteering venture was accompanying Dr Michael Flowers and his wife June, members of our church and both former missionaries in Bangladesh. I thought Jane would return exhausted, but she came back glowing! The second element was working with refugee and asylum seeker families in Leeds and Wakefield, producing a pack to help schools include children from these families into the school community – which also involved a 'One World' celebration she led at her school. She went back in August 2003 with the BMS for the third element, to teach for a month in Kolkotta, India, helping street children associated with Mother Theresa.

After this, Jane gained CELTA and TEFL qualifications in 2004 which enabled her to teach English to adults whose first language is not English, with a clear view to serve overseas.

Jane's sabbatical visits were the start of significant overseas service, in some very demanding places, not least dangerous Luanda, capital of Angola, West Africa with BMS World Mission (2006). She was supporting and developing pre-school education projects for 12 weeks, of which we spent much time concerned about the various threats and sometimes audible gun fire, contracting malaria, although she also spent some time cosied up watching 'Dinner Ladies' comedy box sets with BMS volunteer worker, Lynne! Another was 8 weeks in Afghanistan. She travelled the world for work, service and for pure adventure, which is reflected in the Life of Adventures map which Lucy and Laura made for her 70th birthday. From 2005 Jane used her language skills to teach with the Amity Foundation, a Chinese Christian Non-Governmental Organisation, on their intensive Summer English Courses, for eleven consecutive summers, supporting groups of Chinese Teachers of English with their English language and teaching skills. These 3- and 4-week Amity programmes were always based in rural and remote areas of China where the support of native English speakers with a qualified teacher and an excellent volunteer team was greatly valued. She gathered and took people with her on successive trips, including young people, for whom this was a life-changing experience, from MBC and via the Friends of the Church in China organisation. Jane has led teams of volunteer teachers to several Provinces in China-Sichuan, Hebei, Jiangsu, Anhui, Gansu, Inner Mongolia, and Guanxi Autonomous Region.

Her impact was great, such that she received a Chinese name, Chen Jing, given on one of her many Teaching visits. This means 'calm'. I know that this was not simply a description of her personality (and I don't remember Jane ever panicking about anything) but it was based upon her deep faith and awareness of the goodness and love of God in her life.

After the family was turned upside down by the death of our son-in-law Richard Joyce in 2013 and then his wife, our daughter, Charlotte in 2014

Jane returned to parenting, investing in our grandson, Sam Joyce (then 6 years old) and teaching, as a volunteer I might add, at his primary school in Meanwood. She gave herself entirely to him and he is testament to her love and resolutely steadfast presence in his life.

After retiring from teaching, Jane did not retire but became the Pastoral Care Coordinator, a volunteer role, at her local church, Moortown Baptist Church, where she has been a member for the past 45 years, leading a team of Pastoral Care Workers, solidifying the idea that retirement was not an option for her. She faithfully delivered this in the most difficult pandemic times: getting people out for walks, bringing a stool to sit outside their window to chat, endless Covid testing before going into care homes, and advocating for those in need.

Jane was a wife, a mother of four, a grandmother of seven, a homemaker, a volunteer abroad, and fulfilled lots of other essential roles, not least continuing parenting throughout her life.

Jane's pastoral skills have been much used in coordinating pastoral care in the church in more recent years, and she both led and undertook care of any who had needs. This was particularly challenging through the pandemic years and in associated difficult times for the church, but Jane held fast, with great grace, committed to what God had called her to. She began a ministry initially to encourage our pastoral team, with a Monday Thoughts and Prayers delivered to the team every Monday from April 2020. Jane sought the heart of God for these encouraging writings, often with a theme occuring to her during the night. Many were directly linked to real life experiences, particularly in our family or community. Her first book, 'Encounters and Journeys' covers the period from April 2020 to March 2023. This book, given away to anyone but initially asking for support for Wheatfields Hospice (where Charlotte was a palliative care nurse), has helped many people all around the world. It has been called a 'spiritual hug'! The sequel book was just finished before Jane died - indeed on the day she died, Monday 28 April, she had Phil send out her last item, typically focussing on others, in this case caring for teenagers with cancer).

Jane was diagnosed with a rare breast cancer (triple negative) in April/May 2024. She had aggressive chemotherapy, causing many very debilitating side effects. She had successful surgery in November 2024 - scans following that and a course of radiotherapy all showed clear in the period up to April 2025, when it became clear that the tumour had spread. In mid-April the prognosis was for several months, but Jane's health declined very rapidly from 26 April, and she died in St James's Hospital late on Monday 28 April. She had told us that she knew where she was going, and was not afraid of death. Her final church service was Easter Sunday, at which two people were baptized – and, fittingly, Jane was the 'towel-holder' (one who serves the one being baptized, as they are very significant to them) for Anne, whom Jane had greatly helped. Her final watch of TV was an episode of 'The Chosen' a Christian drama, on Jesus raising Lazurus from the dead, and the anointing of Jesus. The silk painted banner (designed and made by Jane, and some of the children at church) which was laid on Jane's coffin carries the words of Jesus 'I am the Resurrection and the Life':

Jane wrote in the 'about the author' section in her first book : "*God's faithfulness, grace and love has been with her, her husband, and their family throughout these many years. The journey has not always been easy and there have been challenges, and unexpected twists and turns in the road.*

Trust in the Lord with all your heart;
*   do not depend on your own understanding.*
* Seek his will in all you do,*
*   and he will show you which path to take.*
Proverbs 3 v 5-6 TLT
You chart the path ahead of me and tell me where to stop and rest. Every moment you know where I am. You both precede and follow me. Psalm 139 v 3 and 5 TLB. "

Personal notes:

Our son John included these thoughts in his appreciation of his mother at her thanksgiving service:

A celebration of life service seems too final...yet, I think there has been a shared sense from many that this is quite different, that this is not the end but an opportunity, an invitation and a new and more colourful beginning (and mum did love colour!) Having my own kids has given me insight into just how amazingly calm and centred mum was. To handle four kids, a household, some of the most huge spectacles and a full time role in managing a husband called Phil, I marvel at how she managed all with so much grace.

Mum was a quiet calm, a powerful heartbeat that wasn't always at the forefront of everything but she was the beating heart, loving, willing on, being present and available, offering comfort and also always looking up to God with a sense of hope and joy!

She often subtly talked about the power of presence and then wrote about it one day as her Monday Thoughts and Prayers.

Her life is a rich tapestry of colour, texture, hues and designs. Mum lived deeply (from a well of her own experiences) but as a result could share in sorrow or hardship, suffering and celebration. She had a bigger heart than we ever knew and clearly had a God given gift of being able to do so much with her time for God's glory. Mum was constantly attending to the duty of being present. Fighting through life's clutter, to remain constant, stand firm against every wave that she encountered. She was able to stand firm as her faith was so deeply rooted and with God on her side.

Although Mum had many achievements and titles, including, daughter, sister, mum, wife, teacher and many more. I always felt her true title was leader. When you think of a leader, you may have a specific image in mind but I think Mum broke the mould and definitely led by her example. I think she broke the mould, because her leadership was about presence not position.

Mum was fluent

> in compassion,
> In humility,
> In listening,
> In presence.

You will be missed greatly from our own space that you filled so wonderfully...but I take great comfort that you know where you are to go. Love you mum.

Sam's reflections include:

When my mum died, I became Nana's main focus. I've never really fully appreciated that until now. She was generous in every way, but mostly generous with her time. She didn't consider her time for herself, she considered it to be for others. She put so much of her time into helping me that I have no idea how she did it. Her organizational skills were unmatched. I remember comparing her to Monica from Friends (!) From seeing her as this incredible, skilled, caring woman, who even with cancer, helped people who were arguably less ill than her.

Over the course of her illnesss, seeing her gradually weaken was challenging. On the Sunday before the Monday when she was taken to hospital, seeing her be unable to move or stand was like a punch to the stomach. I want her to be remembered as someone who never put herself first even when there was no one in the room. She gave her time to help people, and through us keeping her legacy alive, she can continue to help people more and more.

A personal note from Phil:

This is not the end! I can't express how precious Jane is to me (to us), how much I love her and how greatly I respect her, and I will do all in my power to honour her. She is at rest now after a very difficult year, but a year where she continued to be as focussed as ever on family and others in our church and community. I could not stop her – and would not want to, it was her life. Jane continued every day to follow Jesus, her Lord, and to give herself away to others, being kind to all she met often despite her own pain. I am humbled by such devotion, which I hope encourages all of us to do the same. Her journey here is finished – but the impact of her life will most certainly continue, and grow. We are on a mission to honour Jane! One way you can join us is to do what Jane did, showing the observable love of Jesus. (John 13 v 34,35).

Jane referred to the difficulties of the past year as her own 'journey' which we know was in God's hands, and she was so aware of and thankful for the love and prayers of so many. It also made us so much more empathetic to the journeys for so many who are suffering from cancer.

We received an overwhelming number of appreciations of Jane in letters, emails, cards, notes, social media and video. Through these we have a most moving view of how significant Jane's life, love and care for others has been in the hands of God, with such evidence of her loving impact on so many people at home, in the community and worldwide. We are determined to further honour and remember Jane by various means, one is this second book. We will also collate and share the appreciations and testimonies to share how Jane helped people in so many ways, consistently and persistently even whilst being so ill, demonstrating the love of Jesus. I remain humbled by this, and by the gracious responses we have received which reflect this. It makes me want to follow Jesus like this too, and I pray that we will see much effect in all of our daily lives, and so bring the kingdom of God into our own communities, as Jane did.

I have concluded that she led at least 4 lives:

– her children/grandchildren/family and church; her social work/child protection; her teaching, and her international volunteering, all underpinned by her feet on the ground, active faith in her Lord Jesus, her Father God, and her constant helper, the Holy Spirit.

I am so thankful to God for almost 54 years of happy marriage (yet with many challenges – we know that life is not simple) to this remarkable, special, totally dedicated, ultra-organised and most precious person, doing the many things we felt God called us to, which will continue, at home and worldwide, and having many special times together and with family. We were utterly *together* in our hearts and minds - even when both of us travelled separately to many parts of the world. As I look over pictures and think about the impact of Jane's life, I realise that I have fallen in love with her all over again! Also, even though we were extremely committed evangelical Christians at the start of our walk with Jesus as teenagers, the last several years have seen us find a simpler and deeper faith in him, sharing his love in what we do, following Him.

Jane (& I) loved, amongst many scriptures, the description Jesus gives us of his heart, a heart of complete humility despite being the Lord of all - 'Come to me, all you who are weary and burdened, and I will give you rest. Take my yoke upon you and learn from me, for I am gentle and humble in heart, and you will find rest for your souls. (see Matthew 11: 28-30 above).

'A Lifetime of Adventures', lovingly created by Lucy and Laura,
to celebrate Jane's 70th birthday

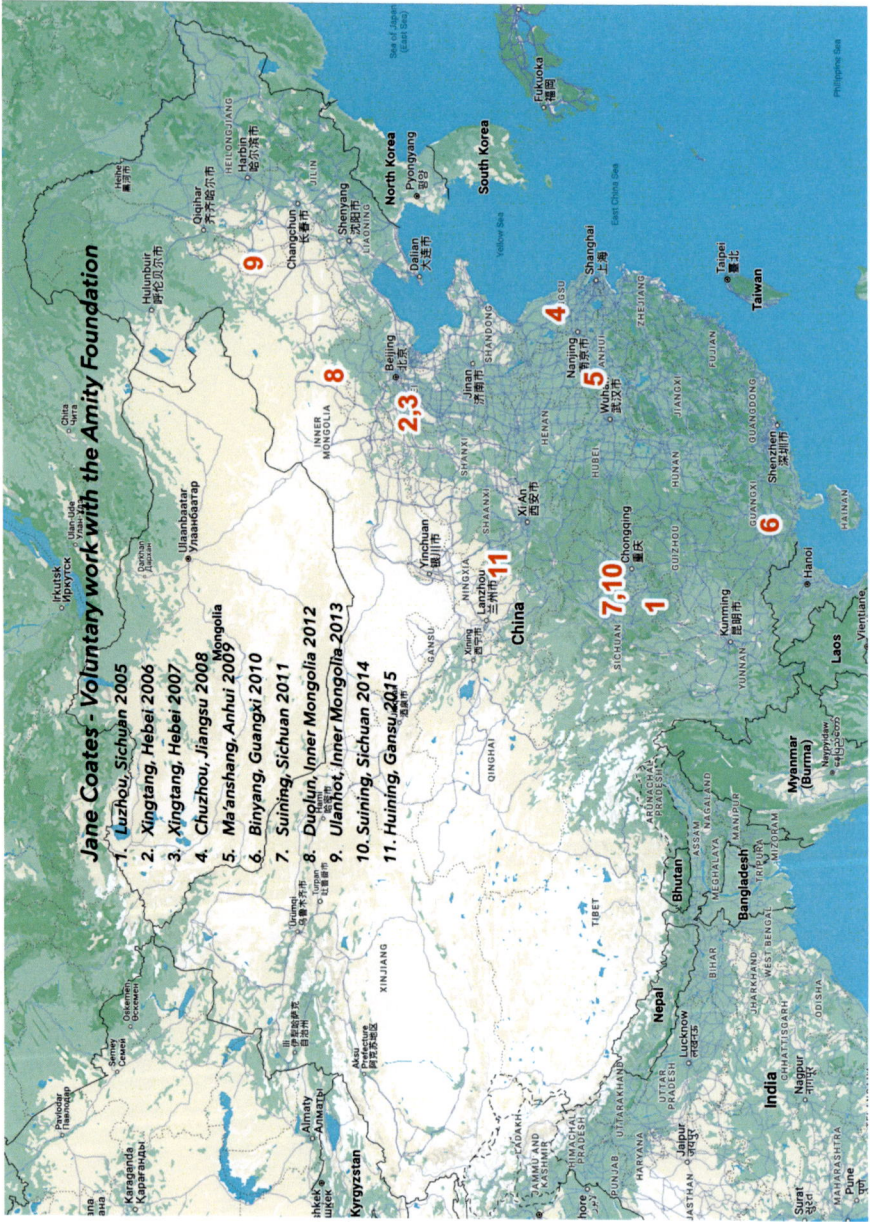

Jane Coates - Voluntary work with the Amity Foundation

1. Luzhou, Sichuan 2005
2. Xingtang, Hebei 2006
3. Xingtang, Hebei 2007
4. Chuzhou, Jiangsu 2008
5. Ma'anshang, Anhui 2009
6. Binyang, Guangxi 2010
7. Suining, Sichuan 2011
8. Duolun, Inner Mongolia 2012
9. Ulanhot, Inner Mongolia 2013
10. Suining, Sichuan 2014
11. Huining, Gansu 2015

Jane's voluntary work with the Amity Foundation, China

陈 静

Chen Jing

Jane's Chinese name, given
to her on one of her visits;
= "calm, still, quiet"
– a very apt description!

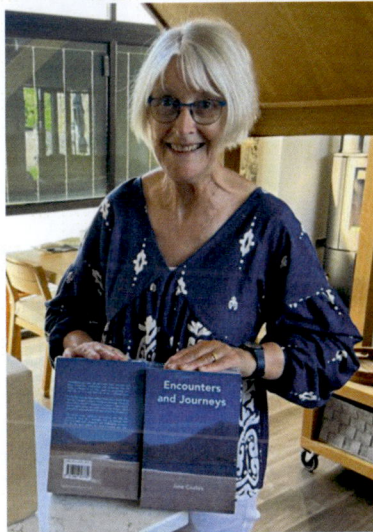

Jane with her first book, Encounters and Journeys

together

with the
grandchildren

hospitality

that smile

19

the fruit of the Spirit is love, joy, peace, patience, kindness, goodness, faithfulness, gentleness

and self-control

Jane & Charlotte

First Thoughts

Children

I began a mammoth task this week sorting through the many, many photograph albums and loose photos that we possess and have collected over the fifty plus years of our marriage, cataloguing the memories and events of the lives of our four children, our many holidays, and then assembling and pasting them into new albums, correctly time sequenced and labelled. Towards the end of the week, I began to wonder why I thought that this was going to be a simple task. But I have had great pleasure in sorting through the photos of our children, remembering their births, mapping their development from baby to child to adulthood and now seeing them with children of their own.

Some of the early photos of the children were in muddled collections of images placed in random envelopes, and as I found myself looking at a photo of a very small girl, and attempting to identify which of our three daughters it could possibly be, I began to realize that this was going to be no quick task. Phil was very amused when I put a photo of our second daughter into the album collection of our first daughter. I had not recognized her! The problem was often compounded by the fact that the same clothes were handed down from our first daughter and then passed on to the second and the third! The T shirt might be the same, but the child was not. But it has been a great pleasure to look through such a vast collection of images and to remember some very special family times.

It has also reminded me of God's great love for His children. He does not make a mistake! There is no confusion with our heavenly Father. He can identify each of his children, He knows them well, inside, and out. He is a good, good Father who delights in each of His children. God has watched us grow into the person that we are today.

Oh yes, you shaped me first inside, then out;
*   you formed me in my mother's womb.*
I thank you, High God—you're breath-taking!
*   Body and soul, I am marvellously made!*
*   I worship in adoration—what a creation!*
You know me inside and out,
*   you know every bone in my body;*
You know exactly how I was made, bit by bit,
*   how I was sculpted from nothing into something.*
Like an open book, you watched me grow from conception to birth;
*   all the stages of my life were spread out before you,*
The days of my life all prepared
*   before I'd even lived one day. Psalm 139 v 13-16 MSG*

Worship Song by Chris Tomlin:

Oh, I've heard a thousand stories of what they think you're like
But I've heard the tender whisper of love in the dead of night
And You tell me that You're pleased and that I'm never alone.

You're a good, good Father
It's who You are, it's who You are, it's who You are
And I'm loved by You
It's who I am, it's who I am, it's who I am.

Oh, and I've seen many searching for answers far and wide
But I know we're all searching for answers only You provide
Cause You know just what we need before we say a word.

But to all who believed him and accepted him, he gave the right to
become children of God. They are reborn—not with a physical birth
resulting from human passion or plan, but a birth that comes from God.
John 1 v 12-13

PRAY
Thank you, God, that I am your child and that I am never out of your sight or your thoughts.

Identity

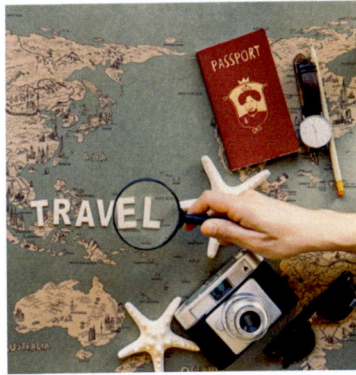

This week I had a frustrating and challenging morning trying to navigate the process of obtaining a new passport for our teenager. There is a 27-page booklet of guidance from the HM Passport Office, with a list of documents that were needed to prove his identity. There was his full birth certificate, an up-to-date photo with countersignature by someone who has known him for several years, and other documentary evidence and declarations to be made. All of this made me think about the subject of identity. Today, our identity is important and must be safeguarded. We have identity documents, our National Insurance Number, our driving licence, and our passport. We are required to have Photo ID to vote and often need proof of our current address. Our phone and its unique number have also become very important as we respond to a request to key in a code to proceed with a payment or to confirm our identity. We may even be asked if we have any distinguishing marks. Our identity is determined by ethnicity, nationality, gender identity, profession and religion and perhaps other significant things too. But what is the essence of my identity? What are the core values and guiding principles that define me, my choices, and my life?

When I consider who I am in Christ then I can get a clearer of my identity from a wider perspective. I am loved, I am chosen, I am redeemed, I am forgiven, I am a child of God, and I am precious in His sight. I am enough. Therefore, we should never lose sight of who we are.

But you are not like that, for you are a chosen people. You are royal priests, a holy nation, God's very own possession. As a result, you can show others the goodness of God, for he called you out of the darkness into his wonderful light.

"Once you had no identity as a people;
*   now you are God's people.*
Once you received no mercy;
*   now you have received God's mercy. 1 Peter 2 v 10 NLT*

Who am I that the highest King
Would welcome me?
I was lost but He brought me in
Oh His love for me
Oh His love for me.

Who the Son sets free
Oh is free indeed
I'm a child of God
Yes, I am.

In my Father's house
There's a place for me
I'm a child of God
Yes, I am.

I am chosen not forsaken
I am who You say I am
You are for me not against me
I am who You say I am
I am chosen not forsaken
I am who You say I am
You are for me not against me
I am who You say I am
I am who You say I am. **Hillsong Worship**

The Transformation Challenge and Pentecost

I am so delighted that the Great British Sewing Bee is back on our screens. In this programme, 12 home sewers are challenged to create ready to wear beautiful garments. Each week the sewers undertake three challenges. In the Pattern Challenge, each sewer chooses a unique fabric but follows an identical paper pattern. In the Transformation Challenge, sewers are given just 90 minutes to turn items of old clothing into something new, wearable, and exciting. This is a test of their creativity, design flair and imagination. Finally, there is the Made to Measure Challenge, where they make a garment of their own design, but which must perfectly fit a real-life model. The judges then choose the sewer who has made the 'garment of the week' and the sewer who has struggled with the tasks leaves the competition.

I love the Transformation Challenges. The sewers take a couple of old, second-hand garments and turn them into a new item of clothing. In past programmes, the contestants have been challenged to remake hammocks into summer wear, turn old denim into a Dolly Parton stage outfit, upcycle two men's shirts into a lady's blouse, transform children's school uniform into playful after school wear, and combine two overcoats to make one stylish coat. The extra challenge is that they only have 90 minutes in which to do this. It is such fun.

But there is a much greater transformation that takes place in the life of the Christian and it is not a 90-minute remake. This transformation takes time as the Holy Spirit works on our heart, our mind, our spirit, our character, our motives, and everything else that we are, to make us more like Jesus. This transformation is more than a modification, an alteration, or a reshaping, but is a process of complete renewal, restyling, and reshaping from the inside out, so that we become the new creation that Jesus wants us to be -to be like Him. What is our part in this transformation process? We need to let the Holy Spirit do His work in our lives and be open to the changes, which may be radical and of consequence.

In this Pentecost season, may we invite the Holy Spirit again to transform us, for His glory.

And we all, with unveiled face, continually seeing as in a mirror the glory of the Lord, are progressively being transformed into His image from [one degree of glory to even more glory, which comes from the Lord, who is the Spirit. 2 Corinthians 3 v 18 AMP

Do not conform to the pattern of this world but be transformed by the renewing of your mind. Then you will be able to test and approve what God's will is – his good, pleasing, and perfect will. Romans 12 v 2 NIV

Awaken my soul, come awake.to hunger, to seek, to thirst
Awaken first love, come awake
And do as You did at first
Spirit of the living God come fall afresh on me
Come wake me from my sleep
Blow through the caverns of my soul
Pour in me to overflow
To overflow

Yes Spirit
Come and fill this place
Let Your glory now invade.
Spirit come and fill this place
Let your glory now invade

Worship Song by Jeremy Riddle

Connect

During the half term school break we travelled to the other end of the country to be with, and to connect with family. Trying to maintain this kind of quality connection can sometimes be challenging, time consuming and problematic in terms of practical arrangements, and costly in terms of the energy that it requires to get everyone together in the same place at the same time. Add in the complications of people travelling long distances with small babies, occupying pre-schoolers and older children with activities in the same group and days out, and feeding everyone into the mix as well, then you can see that it could be easy to give up at the first hurdle. But connection is crucial. We need to touch base, maintain communication, create memories, laugh together, play together, remember past days and events, and build family unit.

Paul had to remind the early Christians to keep meeting together. Discouragement, persecution, challenges, and difficulties had perhaps led some early Christians to avoid meeting and being community. Some individuals had stopped making the effort to be together at the fellowship groups and meetings with other Christians.

And let us not give up meeting together. Some are in the habit of doing this. Instead, let us encourage one another with words of hope. Let us do this even more as you see Christ's return approaching. Hebrews 10 v 25 NIV

I love The Message version which translates this same verse this way.

Let's see how inventive we can be in encouraging love and helping out, not avoiding worshiping together as some do but spurring each other on, especially as we see the big Day approaching.

Paul encourages his readers to 'draw near' to God, to hold fast to their faith, and to continue with that vital role of connection. That regular connection, meeting up, worshipping together, sharing meals, and their formal meetings too, were places where they could encourage each other, and spur each other on.

We come to church and receive from God, but we also come to encourage, to bless and to support others." Love needs stimulation and society. Faith and hope can be practised by a solitary in a hermit's cell or on a desert island. But the exercise of love is possibly only in a community." Robinson

We need to assemble, meet up, worship together, connect. Sometimes, Jesus meets us in one another. Let us do all that we can to keep those connections.

PRAY

God, I like my own company. I like the quiet, the peace and your presence. Sometimes it is too hard to be with the big, noisy group, too challenging, too complex, so many different characters and issues. But we are family. Your church is family. Help me to be connected and to stay connected. Help me to be an encourager and a helper.

Devoted

Author of number One Bestseller
Mud, Sweat and Tears

Bear Grylls
A Survival
Guide *for* Life

How to achieve your goals, thrive
in adversity and grow in character

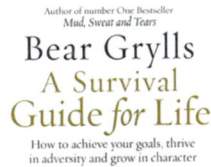

Bear Grylls, the Chief Scout and Christian, has written a book called A Survival Guide for Life -How to achieve your goals, thrive in adversity, and grow in character. We are reading this book with our own teenage scout and the daily readings share the wisdom that Bear Grylls has gleaned from some of life's harshest experiences and environments. One of the significant readings this week was 'to be the most enthusiastic person you know'. "Enthusiasm so often makes the critical difference. It sustains you when times are tough. It encourages those around you. It is totally infectious, and it rapidly becomes a habit. Enthusiasm adds that extra 5% sparkle to everything we do, and life is so often won or lost in that little extra bit that carries us home over the finish line." We are encouraging our own Explorer Scout to be as enthusiastic as possible-in everything he puts his hand to.

Enthusiasm is a wonderful thing. Being wholehearted, devoted, zealous, eager, and passionate about something are attitudes to be admired if that enthusiasm is directed at an appropriate challenge or cause. Saul was one of the most zealous, passionate, devoted, enthusiastic and wholehearted of religious individuals. He was a devoted and zealous Jew and of Judaism with its rules and regulations. But his zeal and passion were misplaced and led him to persecute the Christians and early church. Then he met Jesus, and his life was completely turned around.

For you have heard of my previous way of life in Judaism, how intensely I persecuted the church of God and tried to destroy it. I was advancing in

Judaism beyond many of my own age among my people and was extremely zealous for the traditions of my fathers. Galatians 1 v 13-!4 NIV

After his encounter with Jesus, his devotion and energy took him in an entirely new direction. He also encouraged the early Christians to direct their energies and passion towards Jesus, their fellowship with other believers, and supporting the growth of the early Christian church.

The fellowship of the believers They devoted themselves to the apostles' teaching and to fellowship, to the breaking of bread and to prayer. Acts 2 v 42 NIV.

Love must be sincere. Hate what is evil; cling to what is good. Be devoted to one another in love. Honour one another above yourselves. Never be lacking in zeal, but keep your spiritual fervour, serving the Lord. Romans 12 v 9-11 NIV

We are encouraged to be faithful, devoted and even enthusiastic followers of Jesus. As a young Christian in teenage and early adult years this was my reality. But as family, work and other responsibilities increase, then it can be hard to maintain that same level of involvement, activity, and sheer enthusiasm. But God knows our circumstances, commitments, physical limitations and the like and has a place and a purpose for each of us. Let us have that enthusiasm of the heart for Jesus, for our fellow believers and for His church.

When the elderly King David was handing on the torch to the young Solomon, whom God had chosen to build His Temple, David said,

" And you, my son Solomon, acknowledge the God of your father, and serve him with wholehearted devotion and with a willing mind, for the Lord searches every heart and understands every desire and every thought. If you seek him, he will be found by you; but if you forsake him, he will reject you for ever. 1 Chronicles 28 v 9 NIV

Whatever age or stage we are at, may we love and serve with enthusiasm, in whatever way we can. "Let's be all in so that we can be all out."

PRAY May I have a willing, loving heart to serve you.

Dads and Parents

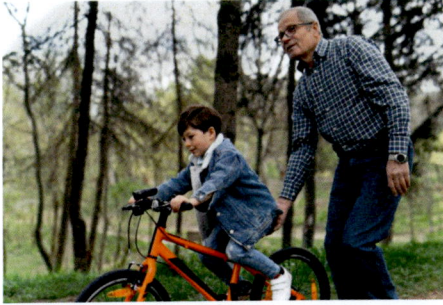

As we celebrate Father's Day again, I have been thinking of the times spent with my dad. I have wonderful memories of my dad and growing up with him and mum who were both amazing and loving parents. I am very fortunate to be able to write those words as there are so many people who cannot say that their childhood was happy, loving, secure and solid.

Our small family of four, dad, mum, my brother, and myself, lived in rented property in a street of terraced houses in an area that was certainly not regarded as affluent or desirable. My dad was always in work as a Compositor/Printer for a Printing Company and so his job was secure although not well paid. My mum stayed at home and cared for the family when we were small and then when we were teenagers, she took on some part time work. We never possessed a car and had just a one-week holiday each year in a Scarborough boarding house. We went back to the same one every year.

My childhood was secure and solid. My dad taught me to fish with a hand line and a rod in both the lake and the sea. He had an allotment and was part of a Horticultural Society and my weekly visit to work on the allotment and take part in the Flower Shows and competitions were an important feature of my life. He loved and grew a massive range of dahlias and fuchsia. We had the early basic types of cameras, but we developed and printed our own photographs in the little chemical baths and makeshift dark room in the cellar of the house. We made matchstick model houses and log cabins using his spent matches and glue. Such simple tasks were time consuming but gave precious time together. Together we made cardboard and wooden puzzles, toys, and games. It was my dad who taught me to ride a bike-running up and down the cobble stone street alongside and then after me. He taught me to play chess with many of the quick, instant saving moves- which I have long forgotten. Dad repaired the family shoes with the cobbling equipment that he had in the cellar and taught me the value of repairing and mending. My dad had a background in the Boys Brigade as a young man, my mum had attended a local Gospel Chapel, and they supported my attendance at the local Anglican church. At the weekend we would go off by bus to one of the local parks.

Dad was a quiet man of few words but still very sociable. The kettle was always on and there was always a cup of tea for a neighbour, friend or family member who called by-which happened very frequently. On Hogmanay, and Burns Night, it felt as if the whole street would descend on our little house. On a Saturday night he would sometimes take me with him to the local club where he played billiards or snooker- but the tables were for adults only and so I never learned to play either game. Dad never raised his voice, or was angry, cross, or bad tempered. In fact, quite the opposite- after a few beers he was hilariously funny.

My parents were loving, generous hearted and giving, and I am so thankful to them. They were solid and I had a solid base. I hope that I have done them justice in my own parenting and grand parenting. As parents we are there to nurture, protect, encourage, inspire, train, develop and to provide a platform and launch pad from which the next generation can fly on their own.

Parents don't come down too hard on your children or you'll crush their spirits. Colossians 3 v 21 MSG

And fathers, don't have unrealistic expectations for your children or else they may become discouraged. Colossians 3 v 21 TPT

And now a word to you parents. Don't keep on scolding and nagging your children, making them angry and resentful. Rather, bring them up with the loving discipline the Lord himself approves, with suggestions and godly advice. Ephesians 6 v 4 TLB

Fathers don't frustrate your children with no-win scenarios. Take them by the hand and lead them in the way of the Master. Ephesians 6 v 4 MSG

Father, being a parent is a tough call. We pray for the parents, grandparents, role models, teachers, youth leaders that we know and ask that they may look to you for wisdom, grace, and patience.

We pray for families separated by war or conflict, for families where a parent may be absent, for blended families, families where there is strife and conflict, family breakdown in its many forms. You are Abba Father and you have compassion on all your children.

Planted-in the right place

We have been establishing a brand-new garden complete with central lawn and borders. Many of the plants were purchased at the Plant Sale over the past two years but as an inexperienced gardener it has been a bit of a hit and miss situation in terms of where plants should be placed. I am usually just glad if I can buy a plant from the Plant Sale or garden centre, put it into the soil, which is not good quality, and it survives. I am happy for survival rather than thriving. But I was assisted in the planting this time by an experienced gardener who guided me with my new purchases. I was instructed as to where each plant should go- sun or shade, pot or ground, spreading habit or tall and bushy, colour themes and contrasts, and I am glad to say that all the plants seem to have settled in their new places. Correct medium, nourishment, water, and light are apparently key factors but another of the key factors is correct location. Correct location means that the plant with receive the correct amount of light and not be overshadowed by the neighbouring, spreading plants.

People, like plants need to be in the right place and have the space and nurture that they require. God is our source of nurture and nourishment and our growing and maturing is a process that has no end point. We are always in the process of growing and developing. If we have stopped growing, then perhaps something is wrong. God wants to continually nurture, sustain, enrich, protect, and move us forward.

Let your roots grow down into him and draw up nourishment from him. See that you go on growing in the Lord and become strong and vigorous in the truth you were taught. Let your lives overflow with joy and thanksgiving for all he has done. Colossians 2 v 7 NLT

Some of my newer plants are in danger of being eclipsed by the established lavender plants that were put in first. Have you ever felt eclipsed by someone or something, swamped, 'put into the shade', disadvantaged whether numerically or in terms of ability? You may have felt that there are more things working against you than for you. This is not a comfortable place to be in.

This week, I joined a Parent and Carers Multi Faith Hub at the very large, local and prestigious school that our grandson attends. The Hub was anxious to have a Christian group who would be the parent contacts for all things Christian and faith activities at the school, link with the Lead Christian member of staff and be a part of celebrating the rich diversity and multi faith nature of the school. As I joined the hub today, with two other Christian women, I felt outnumbered and inadequate. Was I in the right place? Why do I think that I have got a right to be here? The Muslim, Hindu, and Jewish members who attended were far more vocal and full of ideas and suggestions for joint activities and faith celebrations for the whole school community. What could I add? The leader of the group indicated that there were not very many Christians willing to be identified as such within the school parent group. This was a surprise as the school is so large. So, I was feeling insecure, outnumbered, and inadequate. But God is the God of planting, growth, and abundance. He is not the God of lack, and disadvantage.

After all, who is Apollos? Who is Paul? We are only God's servants through whom you believed the Good News. Each of us did the work the Lord gave us. I planted the seed in your hearts, and Apollos watered it, but it was God who made it grow. It's not important who does the planting, or who does the watering. What's important is that God makes the seed grow. The one who plants and the one who waters work together with the same purpose. 1 Corinthians 3 v 6-8 NLT

I close my letter with these last words: Be joyful. Grow to maturity. Encourage each other. Live in harmony and peace. Then the God of love and peace will be with you. 2 Corinthians 13 v 11 NLT

PRAY

Father, I know that you have placed me according to your purpose. I do not need to feel inadequate, useless, outnumbered and overshadowed when your resources are available to me. Help me to have confidence in you and not in my own resources.

Wandering sheep- green pasture or rocky road?

We live in a green belt area, and I am part of a Facebook Group for our local rural area. One of the almost weekly posts on the Facebook link is a photo like the one above with a statement 'there are sheep on the road'. The readers try to get a fix on the location in the image and hopefully the farmer owner will be able to retrieve his wandering sheep. This time the farmer was quite relaxed about his missing sheep, saying that they were three lambs, and they would not go far from the mother sheep- leaving him with time to collect them.

In his prophecy, Jeremiah describes Israel and Judah as lost sheep, abandoned by their shepherds and wandering aimlessly. They had lost track of home, could not even remember where their home, safe pastures and paddock were and were vulnerable.

My people were lost sheep.
*   Their shepherds led them astray.*
They abandoned them in the mountains
*   where they wandered aimless through the hills.*
They lost track of home,
*   couldn't remember where they came from.*
Everyone who met them took advantage of them.
*   Their enemies had no qualms:*
'Fair game,' they said. 'They walked out on God.
*   They abandoned the True Pasture, the hope of their parents.*
Jeremiah 50 v 6-7 MSG

These few verses from Jeremiah really struck home to me. The only safe pasture is with the shepherd. We are very prone to wandering off and leaving our true place and our Shepherd. When we lose sight of the Shepherd, we lose our bearings. When we do not have His presence and His voice, we lose sight of who we are, where we should be and what we should be doing. But the Shepherd always knows where we are and will bring us back. Though God's people were lost, and scattered, Jeremiah's prophesy would give them hope that when they returned to their God, He would punish Babylon, they would return to their homelands, and would be restored.

You were lost sheep with no idea who you were or where you were going. Now you're named and kept for good by the Shepherd of your souls. 1 Peter 2 v 25 MSG

The sheep that are My own hear and are listening to My voice; and I know them, and they follow Me. John 10 v 27 AMP

David, in his shepherd Psalm, knows and declares that His God is a personal God, He is 'my' shepherd. His care for David, and us, is personal. David, as a shepherd, knows that sheep are wanderers by very nature and need the shepherd to guide them. Sheep do not need to know where the green pastures and water supplies are. All they need to know is the presence of their shepherd and that where he is, they will be safe. His presence and his voice will reassure them in every situation.

GOD, the Master, says: From now on, I am the shepherd. I'm going looking for them. As shepherds go after their flocks when they get scattered, I'm going after my sheep. I'll rescue them from all the places they've been scattered to in the storms. I'll bring them back from foreign peoples, gather them from foreign countries, and bring them back to their home country. I'll feed them on the mountains of Israel, along the streams, among their own people. I'll lead them into lush pasture so they can roam the mountain pastures of Israel, graze at leisure, feed in the rich pastures on the mountains of Israel. And I will be the shepherd of my sheep. I will make sure they get plenty of rest. I'll go after the lost, I'll collect the strays, I'll doctor the injured, I'll build up the weak ones and oversee the strong ones, so they're not exploited. Ezekiel 34 v 12 MSG

This is our Jesus, our Shepherd. Let us not wander off from His presence and His voice. I have read that sheep will only lie down if they feel safe, are not threatened by danger, if they have plenty of food, and if they are in the company of other sheep. 'He makes me to lie down in green pastures.' The sheep in the image are lost, on their feet, separated, and away from the shepherd. They cannot lie down in safety.

There is a very ancient hymn, Come thou Fount of every blessing
(Songwriter: Robert Robinson 1758)
Jesus sought me when a stranger, Wandering from the fold of God
He to rescue me from danger, Bought me with His precious blood.

Prone to wander, Lord, I feel it, Prone to leave the God I love.
Here's my heart Lord, take and seal it, Seal it for Thy courts above.

PRAY
Jesus. All I need to know that you are there and to hear your voice. Help

me to stay near to you and not wander off. Where you are, I am safe, fed, and fulfilled. I am one among many, but you know me by name.

Green Pasture

"You are my sheep, the sheep of my pasture, and I am your God, declares the Sovereign Lord." Ezekiel 34 v 31

I apologise for thinking about sheep and fields again. All the windows of our barn conversion look out on to green pastures, grazing land for either sheep, horses, or cattle. The field in front of us is the 'summer field 'for four beautiful horses and we see them happily munching the grass throughout the day and the night. Farmers and shepherds are responsible not just for the nourishment of their livestock but also for the lands that they manage and so we see them moving their animals from one field to another to provide fresh grass, but also respite and regrowth for the fields. For the animals, the pasture provides food, exercise, and rest. For the farmer or shepherd, the field is his key resource that needs to be managed. There are lots of sayings about pasture such as 'being put out to pasture,' 'pastures green', and 'finding pastures new.' But for the Christian we have safe pasture if we keep the Shepherd in view-all the time! He will make sure that we find a place, be cared for, and be able to move freely - if He is within sight. He may move us on and that may be strange and hard, but it will always be for our good.

As I think about the many green fields that have been my pasture, I have been reflecting on how it has been clear that a move was needed. I have often been asked 'how has God guided you?' How have you been sure that you were following Him? I have followed different career paths, have taken different courses and training routes, have taught in many different schools, have moved house several times, have had to make countless decisions with the four children, and have been in three different churches. Each time I have had to consider what to do next, whether to stay or go, which career path is calling etc. Is the time right? Is God prompting me to make a move? There are some very clear markers for me and steps that I need to take before I consider greener pastures.

I consciously 'read' my present circumstances. I may need to logically write a list of pros and cons, a little like a balance sheet. I will talk with Christian friends, I will pray, I will read the Bible and most of all I will wait for the peace of God concerning a given situation. When the circumstances or my level of discomfort with a current situation, conspire to point me in a new direction then I will look to the Shepherd for His guidance- friends, scripture, opportunities, and a way forward. Sometimes the way forward may be closed. I remember three separate interviews for Deputy Headship posts that all came to nothing. The processes and interviews were time consuming, exhausting, and drained nervous energy. I then went in an entirely new direction, initially quite risky and very uncertain, but ultimately fulfilling and that nourished my soul and mind. All the time I know that I can trust God with any mistakes that I might make. He will unravel the things that are not right. I trust Him with the present. I move forward in peace and trust Him with the outcome.

Our Shepherd always has safe, perfect pasture for us.

I am the Door; anyone who enters through Me will be saved and will live forever, and will go in and out freely, and find pasture (spiritual security). John 10 v 9 AMP

I will tend them in a good pasture, and the mountain heights of Israel will be their grazing land. There they will lie down in good grazing land, and there they will feed in a rich pasture on the mountains of Israel. I myself will tend my sheep and have them lie down, declares the Sovereign Lord. Ezekiel 34 v 14-15

Radiant

I prayed to the Lord, and he answered me.
He freed me from all my fears.
Those who look to him for help will be radiant with joy;
no shadow of shame will darken their faces. Psalm 34 v 4-5 NLT

David wrote Psalm 34 from a very dark place and experience. He had fled from his enemies on two fronts, the Philistines and from Saul, and had gone into hiding in the Cave of Adullam. At his lowest point, from the extremes of fear and flight, from feigning madness to escape, and in desperation, David had cried out to God and had written this song of deliverance. "Those who look to him for help will be radiant with joy; no shadow of shame will darken their faces." Radiant with joy. How could David write these words from such a dark place. But joy is not happiness. David trusted his God with his future. Like David, those who know that Jesus is with them in their darkest times, can shine with joy, hope, and inner peace. They may not feel 'radiant' but they will shine. They will reflect the light of the Light of the world.

If you are filled with light within, with no dark corners, then your face will be radiant too, as though a floodlight is beamed upon you. Luke 11 v 36 TLB

As water reflects the face, so one's life reflects the heart. Proverbs 27 v 19

In perhaps an inappropriate comparison and a very different story, you may remember the book Charlotte's Web by E.B. White. The story tells how Charlotte the spider weaves four words of praise into her web for her friend Wilbur the pig, which resulted in the saving of Wilbur's life. Charlotte's spider web words were powerful- 'Some pig,' Terrific', Radiant' and Humble.' With just a few short words Charlotte successfully changed the almost guaranteed fate of the pig. Wilbur, the runt of a litter of pigs had always felt small, insignificant, and had endured negative experiences, but his fortunes were transformed. The words in the web served to make him and others recognise how significant and valued he was. Charlotte encouraged Wilbur, against the backdrop of the word 'Radiant' behind him, to display his joy and happiness to the crowd. His demeanour, actions and behaviour proved to be true reflections of that word radiant.

Hopefully we can shine, be attractive witnesses, and reflect the love light of Jesus. We may not feel 'radiant' but let us hold His love in our hearts.

A Perfect Fit

For you are all children of God through faith in Christ Jesus. And all who have been united with Christ in baptism have put on Christ, like putting on new clothes. Galatians 3 v 26-27 NLT

On Monday I had the privilege of taking Sam into a very posh men's outfitting shop in the Victoria Quarter in the centre of Leeds. As a Christmas gift from a longstanding friend, he had been given a voucher for a private shirt measuring and fitting service, the shirt being made to his exact specifications and measurements. Sam has never even been measured for a suit in this way and so it was a luxurious treat for us both. Sam chose the material for his shirt, the collar and cuff style, sleeve length, the buttons, the darts, the monograms. The measurements needed to be accurate and great care was taken with these along with trying on their 'sized examples'. What a luxury it was! The completed shirt will be a perfect fit for him, and he was so pleased to have this opportunity.

We are to be clothed with Christ and His presence in our lives is to be the perfect fit for us. "Instead, clothe yourself with the presence of the Lord Jesus Christ. And don't let yourself think about ways to indulge your evil desires." Romans 13v 14 NLT

Jesus promised to send the Holy Spirit so that we could be clothed with power. I am going to send you what my Father has promised; but stay in the city until you have been clothed with power from on high.' Luke 24 v 49 NIV

We don't have to manufacture this ourselves but trust that He will clothe us and dress us in that 'full adult faith wardrobe'-not just the shirt! "By faith in Christ, you are in direct relationship with God. Your baptism in Christ was not just washing you up for a fresh start. It also involved dressing you in an adult faith wardrobe—Christ's life, the fulfilment of God's original promise." Galatians 3 v 27 MSG

How do you wash waterproof socks?

Sam had an unfortunate accident at the weekend when he put a garden fork through the walking boot on his left foot, leaving him with a small open fracture of his big toe. There were hospital visits to follow, wound dressing, a Tetanus injection, antibiotics and the dreaded open toed plastic boot that made walking initially challenging, especially climbing stairs, and in the snow. The need for some protection for the wound and to keep the dressing dry was essential, and I was advised that there was such a thing as waterproof socks. Such waterproof socks, according to the accompanying information, were engineered for all extremes, such as extreme outdoor activities and weather conditions. The blurb also claimed that the socks were designed to enhance your performance. We duly ordered these socks, and the leaflet proudly announced that the socks were waterproof in every wet condition, breathable, windproof, durable, with a comfortable, soft feel, had a 4-way stretch, a bamboo lining for moisture control and insulation, protected from blisters, had support zones for the foot, were guaranteed weatherproof, and came with a lifetime guarantee. Basically, the manufacturers and researchers had got every base covered.

The word 'covered' made me consider our 'being in Christ.' Joyce Meyer, a well-known American speaker and evangelist, has a wonderful list of 47 statements or gifts that are ours as Christians. If you search for Joyce Meyer 'Knowing who I am in Christ' then her list should appear first. Joyce wants us to know how amazing our life in Christ can be. As I read through the list again, with its Bible verses, I realized that Jesus has 'got it all covered' by what He has done for us. We are redeemed, chosen, accepted, born again, new creations, forgiven, free, loved, complete, at peace, renewed, strengthened, rooted, conquerors, without blame, and people of hope. By grace we are completely covered, if we trust in Christ. We are in the all-encompassing care of Jesus, and we can be confident that His death and His blood has covered every situation and need that we may have. I am covered.

I have put my words in your mouth
  and covered you with the shadow of my hand –
I who set the heavens in place,
  who laid the foundations of the earth,
  and who say to Zion, "You are my people."' Isaiah 51 v 16 NIV

Blessed is the one whose transgressions are forgiven, whose sins are covered. Psalm 32 v 1 NIV

He will cover you with his feathers,
  and under his wings you will find refuge;
  His faithfulness will be your shield and rampart. Psalm 91 v 4 NIV

The Gate and the Gate keeper

He strengthens the bars of your gates,
and blesses your people within you.
He grants peace to your borders
and satisfies you with the finest of wheat.   Psalm 147 v 13-14 NIV

Some years ago, I had the opportunity to serve on several of the BMS World Mission Short Term Placements. Perhaps the most memorable and significant for me, and where there was also a measure of risk, safety concern, and culture adaptation, were the times spent in Herat, Afghanistan, teaching in the International School, and teaching in the Pre School-Education Projects, in Luanda, Angola.

In Herat, the accommodation was securely behind high walls and there was always a gate keeper on duty, especially at night. Before I left the compound in the morning to walk to school, the gate keeper's job was to open the heavy wooden and barred gate. He would walk down to this gate at the end of a long passageway, look out, then walk to the main road, to check that everything was safe. In the early weeks it was safe to walk alone to school or to go by tuktuk. But on some days, he would have to walk me to the school- a job which he hated as he did not want to be seen by others with a westerner. He would walk a long way behind me. But his main job was to guard that heavy gate to the compound.

In Angola, a nurse, a teacher and I shared a house. My role was to teach in the newly established Pre School-Education Projects (PEP's) placed in Luanda. The PEPs were often a two-hour drive away on dreadful roads. At night, there was a gate keeper at the door of the house. He sat all night in a small marquee in front of the house, and his role was to look out for anything suspicious or any threat. Many of the houses on the road had a similar night guard or gate keeper, and we would often hear them whistling and calling to each other through the night, alerting other guards to any possible threat. His was a nighttime role only, as during the day the driver of the jeep provided the protection needed as we travelled to the different projects in the areas where few westerners would be allowed to go, but where the need for the PEP was greatest.

I remember that heavy wooden gate with its strong bars across, the high walls of protection around the compound and the gate keeper. The gate keepers and guards were essential to safety and a measure of calm and peace of mind.

Psalm 147 begins and ends with the words' Praise the Lord!' It is a psalm which encourages us to praise Him for His protection and care. He is the all-powerful, creative God. Our God is the One who provides for us, gives security, strength, and peace. He strengthens the bars of our gates so that we can always feel safe and secure. He protects those that are within. He grants His peace to our borders

In heaven, there will be no need to lock or guard a gate as the gates will be permanently open. The gates will never be closed. There will be no need to feel unsafe or vulnerable, there will be no darkness but only light.

"The gates of the city will stand open all day; they will never be closed, because there will be no night there." Revelation 21. V 25

But the one who enters through the gate is the shepherd of the sheep. The gatekeeper opens the gate for him, and the sheep recognize his voice and come to him. He calls his own sheep by name and leads them out.

Yes, I am the Gateway. Those who come in through me will be saved. They will come and go freely and will find good pastures. John 10

Transitions

In life, we all experience transitions at some point. Some transitions are planned, some unplanned, some may be related to family events, or even fixed dates in life, such as a coming of age, a graduation or a retirement. Learning to change, adjust, and adapt can be unsettling, confusing, and sudden transitions can leave you in a state of flux. Some family transitions can perhaps be planned for, such as a new baby, a change of career, or house move, but some may come out of the blue and shock, such as an injury, a disability, a separation or divorce. Such a sudden switch can be disabling and stressful. A move to a new country, culture and language, will be initially, equally alarming, as perhaps our linked missionaries will no doubt have found. Any change from one thing to another, from one state or condition to another is tough.

I have enjoyed several changes of career, each transition normally fitting around changing family circumstances or the arrival of the next chid. As the family grew, we moved to larger accommodation and then as the family began to move on into independence, we planned a major downsize. That mega move involving a reduction down of possessions and 'stuff', a major de-clutter aiming for a simpler lifestyle, was a long period of transition as we decided what was essential and necessary. One of the biggest changes was the arrival of a small person into our lives when our own children had long ago moved out and we began a parenting role again with the rounds of swim lessons, play dates, birthday parties, reading schemes, school events, cubs and scouts and a hundred and one other things that we thought we had long finished with. An unexpected transition but one that we encountered with joy. Through all these changes we adapt, grow, and change.

We need to anticipate change and new directions because changes will surely come. How we deal with changes, decisions, new directions, new roles, major upheavals, even disappointments, failures and 'shocks' will be key. We have a Saviour who charts the path ahead of us.

The disciples of Jesus had major transitions in their lives. Andrew, Peter, James and John, were fishermen, working the lake but as followers of Jesus their lives on land would be a sharp contrast. Matthew Levi was a tax collector for the Roman government, hated by his own community, but became a follower of Jesus. Simon, the Canaanite, was known as the Zealot. Such Zealots engaged in politics and anarchy, attempting to overthrow the Roman government and so he may have been a revolutionary. But he was trusted to follow Jesus. Judas Iscariot seems to have served as the treasurer for the group, but John 12:4-6 identifies him as a thief and an embezzler. We are given little information as to the occupations of Philip, Bartholomew, Thomas, Thaddaeus or James, the son of Alphaeus. But this unusual group of men, with their different skills, backgrounds, and characters became faithful followers of Jesus. They faced major life transitions. Paul, a strict Pharisee, and persecutor of early Christins was transformed into a leading Apostle by his experience of Christ. His life transformation and transition were sudden and dramatic.

So, how do we manage change, new directions, and transitions-whether planned or unplanned? Do we stress or trust? The plan of God for our lives is good. We can leave the map in His hands.

Don't let the world around you squeeze you into its own mould, but let God re-mould your minds from within, so that you may prove in practice that the plan of God for you is good, meets all his demands and moves towards the goal of true maturity. Romans 12 v 2 JBP

Song
Through all tho changing scenes of life,
  In trouble and in joy,
The praises of my God shall still
  My heart and tongue employ.

An extravagant love

Wikipedia: Exterior image by Ethan Doyle White

The Crossness Pumping Station is a former sewage treatment plant on the south bank of the River Thames. It was designed by Sir Joseph Bazalgette and built between 1859 and 1865. Its purpose was to deal with the raw sewage from the southern part of London. When it became no longer used for this purpose, it was designated as a Grade 1 Listed Industrial Heritage Site because of its amazing Romanesque architecture and design. It is a masterpiece of engineering with its pumps and steam engines but became famous for its spectacular ornamental cast iron metalwork and original paint colours. It has been described as "a masterpiece of engineering-a Victorian cathedral of ironwork."

Why was a sewage treatment plant designed with such love, care, extravagance and incredibly beautiful interiors? Each detail, down to the specially shaped and coloured external brickwork and ornate balustrades of the central Octagon area, are a delight to behold. It is a masterpiece of work that few people at the time would have witnessed. The sole purpose of this unique and magnificently ornate building was to take London's sewage. The glory of the building and its dramatic interiors concealed this very common function. The Victorian designers took pride in their workmanship, attention to detail, making sure that nothing was common or base. A common theme and desire of Victorian craftsmen and women were to give glory to God and to reflect His glory.

Our Father God is a wonderful Creator, designer. His extravagant love leads Him to create. As we look at our world and the canopy of stars we can stand in awe of Him and worship.

The Lord merely spoke,
*   and the heavens were created.*
He breathed the word,
*   and all the stars were born.*
He assigned the sea its boundaries
*   and locked the oceans in vast reservoirs.*
Let the whole world fear the Lord,
*   and let everyone stand in awe of him.*
For when he spoke, the world began!
*   It appeared at his command.*

Psalm 33 v 6-9 NLT

His love created humankind, each person uniquely formed, His work of art, a masterpiece designed by a loving Craftsman.

For we are His workmanship, His own master work, a work of art, created in Christ Jesus, reborn from above—spiritually transformed, renewed, ready to be used for good works, which God prepared for us before and taking paths which He set, so that we would walk in them, living the good life which He prearranged and made ready for us. Ephesians 2 v 10 AMP

At the close of time, we will see the new heavens, the new earth and the new Jerusalem. Our feet will walk on gold, with no need for sun or moon, for the glory of God illuminates the city, and the Lamb is its light.

Then I saw a new heaven and a new earth, for the old heaven and the old earth had disappeared. And the sea was also gone. And I saw the holy city, the new Jerusalem, coming down from God out of heaven like a bride beautifully dressed for her husband.

The wall was made of jasper, and the city was pure gold, as clear as glass. The wall of the city was built on foundation stones inlaid with twelve precious stones: the first was jasper, the second sapphire, the third agate, the fourth emerald, the fifth onyx, the sixth carnelian, the seventh chrysolite, the eighth beryl, the ninth topaz, the tenth chrysoprase, the eleventh jacinth, the twelfth amethyst. The twelve gates were made of pearls—each gate from a single pearl! And the main street was pure gold, as clear as glass. I saw no temple in the city, for the Lord God Almighty and the Lamb are its temple. Revelation 21 NLT

SONG *So will I (100 Billion X) Hillsong Worship*

https://www.youtube.com/watch?v=C2U7ffUM5Ec

Do not say 'I am only...'

*Dear God please untie the knots that are in my mind,
my heart and my life.
Remove the have not's, the can not's
and the do not's that I have in my mind.*

*Erase the will not's, may not's might not's that may find
a home in my heart. Release me from the could not's, would not's and
should not's that obstruct my life.*

*And most of all, Dear God, I ask that you remove from my mind,
my heart, and my life, all of the 'am not's' that I have allowed to hold me*

back, especially the thought, that I am not good enough
Amen.   *Anonymous*

There are many characters in the Bible accounts who felt inadequate, unworthy, felt too old or too young, who were powerless with words, were unloved, were of the wrong cultural group or nationality, who were childless, or heart broken. There were those who felt that the task that God was giving them was too much and that they were surely not the right person for the job. They did not have the skill set or aptitude for the role. But God reminded them of who He was and His grace.

Jeremiah *"Alas, Sovereign Lord," I said, "I do not know how to speak; I am too young." But the Lord said to me, "Do not say, 'I am too young.' You must go to everyone I send you to and say whatever I command you. Do not be afraid of them, for I am with you and will rescue you," declares the Lord.* **Jeremiah** *1 v 6-8 NIV*

But **Moses** *said to God, "Who am I that I should go to Pharaoh and bring the Israelites out of Egypt?"*

Exodus 3 v 11 NIV

Then **Moses** *went out and spoke these words to all Israel: I am now a hundred and twenty years old and I am no longer able to lead you. Deuteronomy 31 v 2 NIV*

Leah *felt unloved and sidelined.*

When the Lord saw that **Leah** *was not loved, He enabled her to conceive, but Rachel remained childless. She conceived again, and when she gave birth to a son she said, "Because the Lord heard that I am not loved, He gave me this one too. Genesis 29 v31-33*

Hannah *"I am a woman who is deeply troubled. I was pouring out my soul to the Lord. 1 Samuel 1 v 15*

John *"After me comes the one more powerful than I, the straps of whose sandals I am not worthy to stoop down and untie. Mark 1 v 7*

We can perhaps identify with many of the characters in the Bible who felt that they were not up to the mark. But, whenever we feel inadequate, have made a mistake, wonder what on earth we think we are doing, have a crisis of confidence, worry that we have made a wrong choice, feel a failure at our given task, then remind yourself of who you are in Christ. Remember that you are loved, you are chosen, you are forgiven, you are accepted, you have the peace of Christ, and you are His workmanship. He has not finished with you yet.

PRAY

'Oh God of second chances and new beginnings, here I am again'.
Nancy Spiegelberg

God be in my head, and in my understanding.
God be in mine eyes, and in my looking.
God be in my mouth, and in my speaking.
God be in my heart, and in my thinking.
God be at my end, and at my departing.

A Medieval Prayer 1538

Footsteps on the Moon

Sunday 20th July 1969 was a memorable and momentous day. It felt as if the whole world was watching. It was the day of the first moon landing when the Apollo Lunar Module Eagle landed on the moon. On that day, mankind achieved something that many had previously thought to be impossible. You may remember watching Neil Armstrong take his first steps on the moon and then listen to his legendary words, "that is one small step for man, one giant leap for mankind." You may remember seeing the landing crafts trundling over the moon's surface leaving their tyre tracks in the moon's surface. The amazing thing is, that as there is no atmosphere on the moon as there is on earth, there is therefore no wind, rainfall, other atmospheric changes or movement on the moon to disturb those footprints. Those footprints and tyre tracks are still there. Footprints, from more than fifty years ago, are there and will continue to be there.

Thinking again about those footprints made me realize that we all leave our unique footprints. We all make a mark that is visible to others, and which may last for a very long time, and may have a deep impact on others. The phrase, 'the world is watching' is a very significant phrase for me as it reminds me that we are often 'on view' to others. People around us, friends, neighbours, work colleagues, other parents at the school gate, notice and observe our actions and reactions, and make judgements about them. Even people that we do not know at the supermarket, the gym, the garden centre, the library may be silently observing how we speak to others, smile, and conduct ourselves.

As Christians, we may sometimes feel that we are judged more closely and perhaps more harshly than other folk. The world loves to find fault and to criticize. Therefore, the standards that we may hold to can often feel to be higher. We are following in the steps of Jesus and so we reflect Him. When Paul wrote to the young man Titus, he made it clear to him that he had to be above reproach in everything. But not just that, Titus had to demonstrate in his words, his attitudes, his relationships, his walk, the graciousness of Jesus.

"And in all things show yourself to be an example of good works, with purity in doctrine having the strictest regard for integrity and truth, dignified, sound and beyond reproach in instruction, so that the opponent of the faith will be shamed, having nothing bad to say about us.

Let no one disregard or despise you. Conduct yourself and your teaching so as to command respect." Titus 2 v 7-8 AMP

He who walks in integrity and with moral character walks securely, Proverbs 10 v 9

PRAY Jesus, please guide my footsteps. I want to walk faithfully in your footsteps. Wherever I go this week, help me to leave a footprint of love, care and grace, considering the other rather than myself. Amen

Love grows, expands and includes

Phil and I have the privilege of four children-all different, all with different personalities, skills, gifts and sometimes challenges. But as each new child was born and came into the family-our love for each individual child grew and expanded to include the new little person joining the family. The love did not diminish or shrink, and there was not a sharing out, a smaller portion of love for each of the children as if there was only a finite amount of love. Our love expanded, and increased so that each child had a bigger share of love and not a lesser one. This week also saw the birth of our seventh grandchild and once again we witnessed that expansion of love as Eli joined his sister Rosie into a wonderful family of love. With each new child and grandchild life gets busier but the love expands to include all.

By this shall all men know that you are My disciples, if you love one another if you keep on showing love among yourselves. Jesus John 13 v 35

Jesus demonstrated and commended this kind of expanding, all inclusive love-among His disciples and Paul then emphasized this same quality of love in the early church. Paul talks about an increasing love in the new, growing fellowships. As faith was flourishing so the early Christians were growing in love for each other and were seeking the best for each other. Paul encouraged the followers to "think of ways to motivate one another to acts of love and good works."

Dear brothers and sisters, we can't help but thank God for you, because your faith is flourishing and your love for one another is growing. 2 Thessalonians 1 v 3 NLT

Since by your obedience to the truth you have purified yourselves for a sincere love of the believers, see that you love one another from the heart always unselfishly seeking the best for one another. 1 Peter 1 v 22 AMP

PRAY for this quality of love in our families, our community and our church.

Milestones

A milestone is often a significant event in life, and it may begin a new chapter or phase of life. For babies and small children there are developmental markers and milestones as they grow and change. Children move from school to Sixth Form to University and then into the world of work. Individuals may go from being single, to leaving home to marriage and then becoming a family. There may be significant milestones in someone's achievements such as sporting achievements. But as each milestone is reached there is the opportunity for a pause and for reflection. These are significant steps along life's road.

It is helpful to have these markers and times for reflection and perhaps in our Christian lives also, there may be milestones. That first commitment of our life to Christ, growing in a young faith, perhaps being baptized and beginning to take on some responsibilities in a local church. Simon Peter, believed to be that author of 1 and 2 Peter, wrote the following words to new Christians in the hope that they would develop into more mature Christians. He wanted these early Christians 'to grow up.'

Like newborn babies, crave pure spiritual milk, so that by it you may grow up in your salvation, now that you have tasted that the Lord is good. 1 Peter 2 v 2-3 NIV

But then Paul realised that for many of the early Christians there was no observable growth. They were still needing someone to feed them 'milk' instead of 'solid food.' They were needing the basics of the Christian faith when they should be mature in the faith and becoming teachers themselves.

By this time, you ought to be teachers yourselves, yet here I find you need someone to sit down with you and go over the basics on God again, starting from square one—baby's milk, when you should have been on solid food long ago! Milk is for beginners, inexperienced in God's ways; solid food is for the mature, who have some practice in telling right from wrong. Hebrews 5 v 12-14 MSG

Perhaps we need to make a spiritual health check and pause to see where we are in terms of our 'faith milestones.' Like small children, there may be growth spurts in our spiritual development and practices, or we may have plateaued in times of business and additional responsibilities. We may be 'running on empty' or past experiences and have lost that first love and passion for Jesus and His presence. Pause and take stock.

We need each other to help us in our faith journey. We cannot do this on our own. Our friends and our church are vital.

True maturity means growing up "into" Christ

We are not meant to remain as children at the mercy of every chance wind of teaching and the jockeying of men who are expert in the craft presentation of lies. But we are meant to hold firmly to the truth in love, and to grow up in every way into Christ, the head. For it is from the head that the whole body, as a harmonious structure knit together by the joints with which it is provided, grows by the proper functioning of individual parts to its full maturity in love. Ephesians 4 v 14-16 JBP

Passion and Purpose

Whatever may be your task, work at it heartily, from the soul, as something done for the Lord and not for men. Colossians 3 v 23 AMP

And don't just do the minimum that will get you by. Do your best. Work from the heart for your real Master, for God, confident that you'll get paid in full when you come into your inheritance. Colossians 3 v 23 MSG

We recently attended a very formal School Speech Day, with the distribution of prizes awarded to many of the students. Awards are given for the different academic subjects taken at school but there is another prize which is called the School Award for Inspirational Contribution to School Life. This award is for those students who have been involved in school life in a very wide sense-in Music, Choirs, Bands, Scouts, mentoring younger students and being involved in outside of school activities also. These students can inspire others.

The students were addressed by the Headteacher and a visiting Speaker who in her long career had worked for the Foreign Office, Ministry of Defence, been an Advisor to a Prime Minister, a Governor of the BBC, is a Peer in the House of Lords, and who had learned several languages during her illustrious career. But both of their messages to the students emphasized one thing-the importance of 'going with your passion'. They were encouraged to choose the subjects, the courses, and the career path that would 'give them a buzz', that they were fascinated by, and not the things that teachers, parents or peer group would wish you to do. This is a very different message to the one that I received at A level. The path may not the easiest, traditional, may be out of the ordinary, but if it is your passion then you will succeed. It will be the thing that you can put your heart and soul into.

In the words from Colossians, Paul was addressing servants- those who had few rights, choices, or entitlements, if any, but he instructed them to work with heart and soul, as if they were working for their God and not for their masters.

One of the books that has had the greatest influence on me is The Purpose Driven Life by Rick Warren. At the very beginning of his book, Warren states that God uniquely created each person- skills, looks, personality, temperament, abilities, and that each person is created for a purpose. "I am your creator. You were in my care even before you were born. Isaiah 44 v 2. Nothing in our life is arbitrary or accidental. God had very specific purposes for us that would allow us to be fulfilled, secure and happy. He knows our passions. But we must link in with Jesus.

It's in Christ that we find out who we are and what we are living for. Long before we first heard of Christ and got our hopes up, He had his eye on us, had designs on us for glorious living, part of the overall purpose He is working out in everything and everyone. Ephesians 1 v 11-12 MSG

PRAY Father, I am not like anyone else. I don't have to try to be like anyone else. Your design and purposes for me are good. I can trust you with my passions, my heart, and my soul.

All Thinking

I would rather be what God Chose to make me
Than the most glorious Creature that I could think of.

For to be born in God's thought And then made by God
Is the dearest, grandest, and Most precious thing
In all thinking.

C. S. Lewis

Fresh Light on the Familiar: My burden is light

You may have seen the new BBC advert for Children in Need 2024 called 'The Heaviest Backpack' which carries a very moving and poignant message. The advert raises awareness of the fact that some children carry around with them additional worries and problems that can feel like a huge weight on their backs, that is always present, with the weight and the burden always with them, and wherever they go. The campaign aims to raise awareness and deliver resources to help parents and trusted adults to relieve some of the burden for children and open a nationwide conversation around children's wellbeing and mental health. The advert can be found on YouTube if you haven't seen it.

One morning I was praying while lying in bed -something that I rarely do I must add-and I had the most tangible, physical feeling of not being able to get up from that prostrate position. The advert 'The Heaviest Rucksack' must have been on my mind, as I began to empty and offload all the worries and concerns, I had, one by one, visualising and naming each thing, as I handed it over into the care of Jesus. I was emptying my personal rucksack of concerns, possibilities, weights and worries. Once I had named all these things then I could get up.

I am so thankful that we have a Saviour who will not lay anything heavy, burdensome or ill-fitting on us. He wants us to live freely and lightly. We can rejoice in this. May we also look out for others who may be carrying burdens and worries that we know nothing about.

"Come to me, all of you who are tired from carrying heavy loads, and I will give you rest. Take my yoke and put it on you, and learn from me,

because I am gentle and humble in spirit; and you will find rest. For the yoke I will give you is easy, and the load I will put on you is light."
Matthew 11v 28-30 NIV

"Are you tired? Worn out? Burned out on religion? Come to me. Get away with me and you'll recover your life. I'll show you how to take a real rest. Walk with me and work with me—watch how I do it. Learn the unforced rhythms of grace. I won't lay anything heavy or ill-fitting on you. Keep company with me and you'll learn to live freely and lightly." MSG

The planting of the Lord, that He may be glorified

The Spirit of the Lord God is upon me to grant to those who mourn in Zion the following: To give them a turban instead of dust on their heads, a sign of mourning, The oil of joy instead of mourning, The garment, expressive of praise instead of a disheartened spirit. So, they will be called the trees of righteousness, strong and magnificent, distinguished for integrity, justice, and right standing with God, the planting of the Lord that He may be glorified. Isaiah 61 v 3-4 AMP

This week I have visited two very beautiful gardens. Magdi, a good friend, and an expert gardener, has an established and beautiful garden. It has been presided over with love and care over many years. Years of planning, designing, purchasing plants, building up the borders, labouring and digging and using her knowledge of all kinds of plants trees, shrubs and flowers.

The second garden is only just beginning but the plans, layout and young plants are all there ready and waiting. This second garden is the Reflection Garden with its Memory Tree, at The Sue Ryder Wheatfields Hospice, Headingley, designed by Kathrine Holland, who had won a Gold Award for her Sue Ryder Garden at Chelsea this year. I was privileged to be at the opening launch of Kathrine's new garden, to speak with her and to hear about the planting that she has established. As an expert gardener, her plans and planting are truly astonishing. Kathrine just needs the rain and the good weather for the plants to thrive and grow over the summer. But, in time it will be spectacular.

I am reminded by these wonderful words from Isaiah, that we are the planting of the Lord, the ultimate gardener. His plans are perfect, His design incredible, placing each person where He needs them to be, so all will flourish and grow together, to make the most beautiful display of His love and grace. The purpose of this, is that we should bring glory to Him. May we be content with where we are planted- light or shade, winter or summer, small under a bush or tree, full of blousy colour or simple variegated greens, tough, and hardy or sensitive and needing care, seed, sapling or tall tree, the gardener knows best. May we be a well-watered garden.

"I am the true vine, and my Father is the gardener." John 15 v1 NIV

The Lord will guide you always; he will satisfy your needs in a sun-scorched land and will strengthen your frame. You will be like a well-watered garden like a spring whose waters never fail. Isaiah 58 v 11 NIV

He asked her, "Woman, why are you crying? Who is it you are looking for?" Thinking he was the gardener, she said, "Sir, if you have carried him away, tell me where you have put him, and I will get him." John 20 v 15 NIV

Graves Into Gardens Song by Brandon Lake and Elevation Worship

You turn mourning to dancing, You give beauty for ashes
You turn shame into glory, You're the only one who can

You turn graves into garden, You turn bones into armies
You turn seas into highways, You're the only one who can
You're the only one who can

Oh, there's nothing better than You There's nothing better than You
Lord, there's nothing Nothing is better than You.

Light

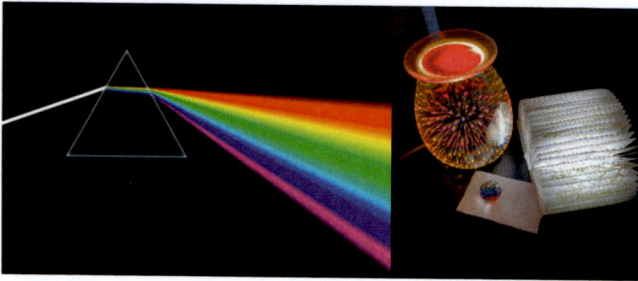

He wraps himself in light as if it were a robe, spreading out the sky like a canopy, Psalm 104 v 2 NIV

You're a fountain of cascading light, and you open our eyes to light. Psalm 36 v 9 MSG

Children are fascinated by light, rainbows and colour. The concept of light is challenging for small children, especially the idea that white light can be separated into rainbow colours, or even bent by passing the light through a glass prism. Yet, when I was teaching in primary school, the children loved to explore and have fun with different shaped prisms, making rainbows. The scientific explanation of different wavelengths or colours of light being refracted or dispersed by different amounts, causing them to separate, coming out of the prism at different angles, creating that wonderful spectrum, was often way beyond them. That would come later. But for now, it was fun to make rainbows.

We have some wonderful colourful light objects at home which delight the grandchildren. A multi-faceted glass crystal, a multicoloured lamp, and a magic book that opens with different kinds of light. These things delight and give joy.

Our early understanding of the God who created light from nothing, and Jesus as the Light of the world, are perhaps childlike in some ways. Some concepts are very hard to grasp. I love the description of our Creator God in Psalm 104, a Psalm which is very reminiscent of the Genesis creation account. Our Creator God wraps Himself in light. He made moon to mark the seasons, and the sun that knows when to go down. He set the earth on its foundations; and the land is satisfied by the fruit of his work. He is a fountain of cascading light.

We are now the children of light, and we live in the light of Christ. "You yourselves used to be in the darkness, but since you have become the Lord's people, you are in the light. So, you must live like people who belong to the light." Ephesians 5 v 8 GNT

The God who said, "Out of darkness the light shall shine!" is the same God who made His light shine in our hearts, to bring us the knowledge of God's glory shining in the face of Christ. 2 Corinthians 4 v 6 GNT

May we reflect the light of Jesus, as children of light. May our words and lives be attractive, winsome, so that others notice something rather different in us and be attracted to the source of that light and energy. May our lights shine in the shadows and the dark places. May our lights point out the way for others.

A Celtic Circle Prayer

Circle me Lord, Keep hope near, And evil afar."
Circle me Lord, Keep light near, And darkness afar."
Circle me Lord, Keep peace within, Keep fear out."
Circle me Lord, Keep hope within, Keep doubt without.
Mighty God, My protection be Encircling me.
You are around My home, my street Encircling me
O Sacred Three

Resources for the Journey

Sam is undertaking 3 different expeditions over the summer. The first of the expeditions is a three-day Duke of Edinburgh Silver challenge around Ilkley and the Yorkshire Dales. The second challenge takes him to the scout camp at Ashness, the Lake District, and the third expedition is to the International Scout Camp in Switzerland. The three camps are quite different in character, in length, and require very different resources. The Duke of Edinburgh expedition requires plenty of high calorie, instant food, several water bottles, and light weight kit, as the rucksack carries three days of kit, including the tent, all carried on his back. The eight-day Scout Camp in the Lake District requires plenty of insect and mosquito repellent, more changes of clothing and plenty of wet weather gear. The ten days international camp in Switzerland requires complex travel arrangements, walking poles, sun cream, swim gear, and lots of changes of clothing. The requirements, the purpose, the resources, the number of students involved, and the size of the rucksack for each of the camps are different. The one requirement that all three camps share is a generous number of good walking socks! The kit lists for the camps are quite specific and detailed.

The Duke of Edinburgh is a personal challenge. The Lake District camp is a leadership training opportunity, and the Switzerland International Centre will deliver exciting challenges meeting scouts from many world countries.

On our Christian journey through life, we have different seasons and times. Some of these times are intense, busy, challenging, and perhaps exciting, and some of our seasons and challenges may require a more evenly paced, even slower step, and a different set of resources. But we need those resources in our backpack, whether that is a 20-litre backpack or a 65-litre holdall. God is our provider and' resource-er', and He knows what we need to accomplish any goal, or deal with any challenge.

There may be times when we can run, climb that summit, and move at that brisk pace unhindered, but there may also be times when we need to saunter, rest at the viewing platform, and consciously slow down for a while. God knows what we need at each point and phase, and His resources are there ready and waiting. He is going to provide the resources that we need in every circumstance.

And my God will meet all your needs according to the riches of his glory in Christ Jesus. Philippians 4 v 19 NIV

And my God will liberally supply, fill until full, your every need according to His riches in glory in Christ Jesus. AMP

You can be sure that God will take care of everything you need, his generosity exceeding even yours, in the glory that pours from Jesus. Our God and Father abounds in glory that just pours out into eternity. MSG

Grow your Gift

We are Legal Guardians and Trustees for a grandson, and we manage the assets and money that were set aside for him many years ago. Everything that we do as Trustees is done for him, and in his, the beneficiary's, best interests. We safeguard those interests and assets, and we cannot benefit from them in any way ourselves. As Trustees, there are many responsibilities, but everything that we need to do, prioritizes his needs and welfare. So, it was with interest that I read the following verse in 1 Peter declaring that we are trustees of God's multi-faceted grace and a steward of His gifts.

As each of you has received a gift, a particular spiritual talent, a gracious divine endowment, employ it for one another as befits good trustees of God's many-sided grace, faithful stewards of the extremely diverse powers and gifts granted to Christians by unmerited favour. 1 Peter v 10 AMP

This verse is so rich in meaning. First, it declares that we each have been given a talent, a specific gift, a spiritual gift, a gracious endowment, that is to be used for the benefit of others. Our Father God has a whole range of wonderful gifts and graces that He grants to believers through His unmerited favour and love. There is no exception. You are gifted and graced with something that He wishes you to use for the benefit of all. It is something that is special to you.

Secondly, we are trustees and faithful stewards of His grace and of the gift, or gifts, that we have been given. I am a trustee of His grace and so my priority is to look beyond myself and outwards towards the other. The needs and welfare of others, and especially those of the household of faith, should be my first consideration even though this may be costly at times. In a simpler translation it says, *"God has given each of you a gift from His great variety of spiritual gifts. Use them well to serve one another. NLT*

If you are not sure as to what your special gift or grace is, then ask a close friend. They will have recognized It, if they know you well. Do not be embarrassed to ask them. We are talking about gifts-something 'given. Your special gifts and grace are needed in your family, your fellowship, and your community. It is a gift that you have received and so do not hide it away. 'Grow your gift' and in this way God's kingdom will also grow.

PRAY
Father, You are blending us together, for your purpose. Everyone is

needed, everyone valued, everyone gifted, everyone included. Help us to recognize the gifts in each other. No-one overlooked.

Knitting, Fishing and Connection

This powerful drawing, by Anja Rozen, a 13-year-old primary school student in Slovenia, is called, 'we are all connected.' From 600,000 international entries from children and young people, Anja's work was chosen as the winning piece, of the International Plakat Miru competition in 2020-2021, illustrating the theme of peace. Anja, an enthusiastic knitter, may have drawn inspiration from her other passion, knitting, for the idea for this striking piece of artwork.

"My drawing represents the land that binds us and unites us. Humans are woven together. If someone gives up, others fall. We are all connected to our planet and to each other, but unfortunately, we are little aware of it. We are woven together. Other people weave alongside me, my own story; and I weave theirs." Her illustration encourages us to be more conscious of our relationships with one another, fostering that sense of community and shared purpose that is so essential in our search for peace and harmony. Anja Rozen may inspire us to safeguard our connections and strive for a more peaceful and cohesive world.

I spotted Anja's artwork when Nathan's Sunday morning message, 9th March, about net fishing as opposed to line fishing, was still much in my mind. I could visualize a large group of people holding securely on to their part of the fishing net, not willing to drop their hold of the net's edge, for fear that the contents could be lost. The net needed to be held firm by each person. Each person is valued and I need to look after the people to my right and left, and they need to look out for me. We are community together and we are looking out for others to come alongside to hold on to the net and to gather in the fish. I need others to strengthen my hands when they become weak, and my grip might weaken. We need the strong people to launch the net. We need those who are wise leaders to read the weather and the water currents, to know where the fish are likely to be, who can interpret the signs and know when to launch, close the net, and secure the catch. We need skilled crafts people to repair the net should it be weak or torn.

I used to play a cooperative game with my school students called 'the web of strength.' In this game, everyone stands in a circle and one person starts making a web with a ball of yarn or string. The first person shares a personal strength (e.g., "I'm good at listening"), and throws the ball of string to someone else across the circle. The process continues until everyone has shared a thought or a strength and is connected by the string The end result is a spider's web of string across the circle. The physical web symbolizes how the students are all interconnected, how they can see their own and others' strengths and weaknesses and value and support each other.

Connection is vital.

Christ—from whom the whole body, joined and knit together by what every joint supplies, according to the effective working by which every part does its share, causes growth of the body for the edifying of itself in love. Ephesians 4 v 16 NKJV

Steps

A man's heart deviseth his way: but the Lord directeth his steps. Proverb 16 v 9 KJV   Within your heart you can make plans for your future, but the Lord chooses the steps you take to get there. TPT

Go ahead and make all the plans you want but it's the Lord who will ultimately direct your steps. We are all in love with our own opinions convinced they're correct, but the Lord is in the midst of us testing and probing our every motive. Before you do anything, put your trusts totally in God and not in yourself. Then every plan you make will succeed. The Lord works everything together to accomplish His purpose. Even the wicked are included in His plans. When the Lord is pleased with the decisions you've made, He activates grace to turn enemies into friends. TPT

A man's mind plans his way as he journeys through life,
But the Lord directs his steps and establishes them.   AMP

Two men, thirty miles apart, called by name

I have often been aware of meeting someone or connecting with someone who seems to have been brought into 'my orbit' or linked with our family, at just the right time. The timing of the meeting or the connection, just seems to happen at the most perfect time. This feels to be a 'God thing.' It just feels to be right somehow- the perfect timing and the most supportive and significant of meetings and connections. As I read in Acts 10 there is one such God meeting where God speaks to two individuals, who would have no obvious connection, opposites in so many ways, in two unique ways, at a precise time, calling each by name and bringing them together, with the most significant consequences for the early church.

Cornelius is a Gentile, from Caesarea, the Roman city on the shores of the Mediterranean in Judea, and the headquarters of the Roman governor of the province of Judea. "There was a man in Caesarea by the name of Cornelius, a centurion in what was called the Italian Regiment. He was a deeply religious man who reverenced God, as did all his household. He made many charitable gifts to the people and was a real man of prayer. About three o'clock one afternoon he saw perfectly clearly in a dream an angel of God coming into his room, approaching him, and saying, "Cornelius!" Acts 10 v 2 JBP God was getting his attention and giving clear, exact instructions.

Simon Peter is a Jew, a Jesus disciple, and an apostle. Peter was in Joppa staying with "Simon the tanner, whose house was by the sea." and Cornelius was instructed to send for him, and to invite him to come to Caesarea. At the exact time that Cornelius had dispatched his men to search out Peter, God spoke to Peter in a vision. Peter's vision was of a sheet being lowered down to him, full of animals and creatures that were not permitted to be eaten as they were considered unclean. The word to Peter was. "Get up Peter. Kill and eat." "While Peter was still thinking about this confusing vision, the Spirit said to him, "Simon, three men are looking for you. So, get up and go downstairs. Do not hesitate to go with them, for I have sent them." Simon invited his gentile visitors in, offering overnight hospitality, and then travelled with them the following day to Caesarea. The Spirit's instructions were clear and despite any reservations about the Jew/Gentile prohibitions, Peter went with them.

The outcome of this amazing God choreography was that Peter preached Jesus to Cornelius and those gathered with him heard the Jesus message. Cornelius and his household became believers, received the Holy Spirit and were baptized as Gentile converts. Peter realized that God was calling Gentiles into His kingdom on an equal footing with Jewish believers. There was no difference, no discrimination or partiality. Noone is unclean or excluded but all are welcomed and fully accepted into the Jesus family. This was a major turning point for the young church.

Two men were brought together to further God's purposes on that day. "I think angels watched that house that night, with the despised tanner a fellow disciple, the great apostle, and the three Gentiles as they lodged there." (Morgan)

Arise, shine; for your light has come! And the glory of the LORD is risen upon you. For behold, the darkness shall cover the earth, and deep darkness the people; but the LORD will arise over you, and His glory will be seen upon you. The Gentiles shall come to your light, and kings to the brightness of your rising. Isaiah 60 v 13

Jesus also promised, *if I am lifted up from the earth, will draw all peoples to Myself.* John 12 v 32

PRAY

For family and friends who do not know Jesus that God may place someone in their orbit who will influence and attract them towards Jesus.

Be thankful for our Christian friends and influencers.

Emerging Leaders

I remember a programme called 'Jigsaw' some years ago which helped the members of church fellowships to look honestly at the natural and God given gifts that individuals had available to them, to help them to find their place in the church. The emphasis of Jigsaw was that each and everyone had a place and purpose in the church to build up the body of Christ. No exceptions. So, as I have been reading on in Acts, I see the emergence of gifted leaders, each unique, and each with their special place in the early church.

I love the transformation of Peter from the hot headed, feet in first, act before thinking and speaking man, to the person that we read about in Acts Chapter 11 who carefully, logically, calmly, step by step, precisely, gives an account to the Jerusalem 'Circumcision Party of Jews' as to why Gentiles were now included. This Circumcision party had found fault with Peter about the conversion of Cornelius and other Gentiles, and their inclusion into the circle of faith, and they had a 'hostile spirit, opposed, contended and disputed with Peter' and were refusing to consider Gentiles for inclusion into the church. 'But Peter began at the beginning and explained to them step by step, the whole list of events.' Verse 2 AMP Here is a different Peter. Peter the defender, careful, logical, calm, patient, explaining step by step, in detail, the route that God had taken him on, and God's confirmation of His love and impartiality in including all. The result. Prejudice and tradition were overturned. 'When they heard this, they were quieted and made no further objection. And they glorified God, saying, Then God has also granted to the Gentiles repentance unto real life after resurrection.' v 18 As a consequence of this decision, even more Gentile Christians were added to the young church, the word spreading to the Greeks of Cyprus, Cyrene, Antioch and beyond and the first believers being called Christians, 'Jesus People,' at Antioch.

So now, Barnabas comes on to the scene, despatched by that same Jerusalem church, to Antioch, a very significant city, now in Turkey. Barnabas would remain in Antioch for a year to teach and establish the young church there.

'Men from Cyprus and Cyrene, went to Antioch and began to speak to Greeks also, telling them the good news about the Lord Jesus. The Lord's hand was with them, and a great number of people believed and turned to the Lord. News of this reached the church in Jerusalem, and they sent Barnabas to Antioch. When he arrived and saw what the grace of God had done, he was glad and encouraged them all to remain true to the Lord with all their hearts. He was a good man, full of the Holy Spirit and faith, and a great number of people were brought to the Lord. Acts 11 v 20-24 NIV

We know Barnabas as the great encourager. Barnabas saw the grace of God at work. But perhaps he also realized that the task was huge and so he searched out Saul to join him. No need to hold centre stage or to be seen as the important one. The load was shared. Paul joined Barnabas for the year, working together to establish the young church.

I love how these men had very different roles to play. The new steadiness of Peter expounding and spelling out clearly the reasons for their hope in Christ, and for the open access to all who would choose to believe. Barnabas, the encourager, the 'establisher', who was there to build up, strengthen and teach for a whole year. Then Saul would find his place, as a gifted orator, with his knowledge, learning, and gifts, with his God given words and powerful messages.

PRAY.
For those in our church and fellowships to find their rightful place. May God use each person in a unique way to bring glory to Him.

Thoughts from New York

The Survivor Tree

Just before Christmas we had the opportunity to spend a week in New York, with one key visit to the 9/11 Memorial site, formally Ground Zero, and the new World Trade Centre building. Ground Zero is now a commemorative space called "Reflecting Absence," which includes two reflecting pools of water built in the footprints of the former Twin Towers. In the memorial gardens proudly stands the survivor tree. This Callery pear tree was discovered at Ground Zero in October 2001 and although it was severely damaged, with burned and broken branches and damaged roots, it had hopeful signs of life. It was nurtured back into life and now each Spring, the tree bursts into life with the most amazing blossom. It stands in the Memorial site as a living image of recovery, resilience, and survival.

There are some wonderful, encouraging words in the Bible, which compare the believer to being like trees, standing strong, with nourishing roots, and being resilient and thriving in all circumstances.

"But blessed are those who trust in the LORD
*   and have made the Lord their hope and confidence.*
They are like trees planted along a riverbank,
*   with roots that reach deep into the water.*
Such trees are not bothered by the heat
*   or worried by long months of drought.*
Their leaves stay green,
*   and they never stop producing fruit. Jeremiah 17 v 7-8 NLT*

But I am like an olive tree, thriving in the house of God. I will always trust in God's unfailing love. Psalm 52 v 8 NLT

They are like trees planted along the riverbank,
    bearing fruit each season.
Their leaves never wither,
    and they prosper in all they do. Psalm 1 v 3 NLT

The survivor tree only recovered because of the commitment and care of a team of gardeners who nurtured it back into life and health. I am aware that there are many people around us today, who perhaps like that tree, are vulnerable, who have been damaged by life in some way, who may feel to have been marginalised, or broken by their circumstances. These folk need others to come along side and offer care and nurture to bring them back into a place of stability and growth. The human spirit is remarkably resilient but that extra love, support, care, practical help, and patient presence go a long way to helping someone back into a good place.

May we be strong, but may we also look out for others.

The Tower and a 360-degree view

The name of the Lord is a strong tower. The man who does what is right runs into it and is safe. Proverbs 18 v 10 NLV

The One world trade Centre or Freedom Tower was built to replace the Twin Towers destroyed in the attacks of 9/11 in 2001. This beautiful new building was opened in 2018 and at a symbolic 1,776 feet tall (1776 being the year of America's independence), One World Trade Centre is the tallest building in the United States with 104 stories. The top three floors are the One World Observatory, an observation deck open to the public which offers visitors panoramic views of New York City below. The ride to the top in one of the Skypod elevators takes only 47 seconds and shows the journey of New York City from green fields to today's remarkable forest of skyscrapers. Thousands of visitors from all over the world come to visit this most amazing of New York's attractions.

There is a tower, the Tower of Babel, referred to in Genesis, historically very early in the Bible accounts, and for which there is archaeological evidence. But this tower was built out of pride, for fame, in independence of and separation from God. The people used bricks and mortar to create a permanent structure which would reach up to the heavens.

They said to one another, "Come, let's make bricks and fire them well." They used brick for stone and tar for mortar. Then they said, "Come, let's build ourselves a city and a tower that reaches Heaven. Let's make ourselves famous so we won't be scattered here and there across the Earth." Genesis 11 V 3-4 MSG

But God in his mercy had a very different plan for their tower and for their pride and arrogance.

One World Tower is certainly a very beautiful building and today hundreds and thousands of people, people, of many different languages, visit the tower and the Observatory from all over the world. It is almost a reverse Babel. Although the tower reaches into the sky, it is our faithful God who sees all, has that 360-degree view of all things, and is our safe tower of rescue and strength. It is interesting that there is an organisation called *Babel Undone*, with a regular podcast, which encourages the use of advanced modes of communication to improve connectivity between Christians. They seek to celebrate differences while recognising a shared humanity, to undo divisions and create space for Christians worldwide to better understand and learn from each other.

O God, listen to me! Hear my prayer! For wherever I am, though far away at the ends of the earth, I will cry to you for help. When my heart is faint and overwhelmed, lead me to the mighty, towering Rock of safety. For you are my refuge, a high tower where my enemies can never reach me. David - Psalm 61v 1-3 TLB

The Oculus- a symbol of hope

The Oculus, at the World Trade Centre in New York, is a stunning and beautiful piece of architecture. Its functional role is that of a transportation hub and shopping complex with 12 subway lines, the World Trade Centre PATH station, numerous shops, farmers markets, art exhibitions, musical performances and more. Over a million people every week come through this hub. Designed by Santiago Calatrava, the structure was intended to embody a powerful concept of hope and resilience, rooted in the tragedy of 9/11. The elegant, white, metal structure is intended to portray a bird about to take flight from the hands of a child and is seen as a symbol of hope, release, and resilience in the face of every adversity and obstacle.

Here is the science bit. Apparently, the Oculus building is in alignment with the sun's solar angles and there is a small opening in the roof of the Oculus, a skylight, through which the sun shines through. Each September 11, from 8:46 a.m., when the first plane struck, until 10:28 a.m., when the second tower collapsed, this central skylight in the roof matches perfectly with this alignment and the floor of the Oculus becomes flooded with a beam of light.

Such symbols of hope are powerful. It made me go back to the Old Testament again and to read the account of Noah, the ark of rescue, the receding waters, the rainbow as a covenant sign of hope, and the release of the dove from Noah's hands.

He (Noah) also released a dove to see if the water had receded and it could find dry ground. But the dove could find no place to land because the water still covered the ground. So, it returned to the boat, and Noah held out his hand and drew the dove back inside. After waiting another seven days, Noah released the dove again. This time the dove returned to him in the evening with a fresh olive leaf in its beak. Then Noah knew that the floodwaters were almost gone. He waited another seven days and then released the dove again. This time it did not come back. Genesis 8 v 8-12 NLT

As we read and watch the TV news, we know that there is evidence of wrong, evil intention, the overuse of power and the destruction of others. God sees and knows. *"I will never again curse the ground because of the human race, even though everything they think or imagine is bent toward evil from childhood. I will never again destroy all living things. Genesis 8 v 21 NLT*

There are always signs of hope. Let us continue to look towards the light that comes streaming through and sometimes when we least expect it.

Love does not delight in evil but rejoices with the truth. It always protects, always trusts, always hopes, always perseveres. 1 Corinthians 13 v 6-7 NIV

The Statue of Liberty

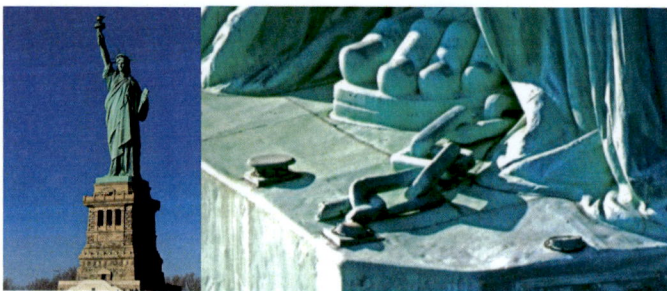

My chains fell off, my heart was free,
I rose, went forth, and followed Thee.
(From the hymn And can it be by Charles Wesley)

The Statue of Liberty is perhaps one of the most familiar landmarks that comes to mind when you think of New York. Lady Liberty stands as a symbol of equality, freedom, and democracy. Most people who visit the statue will do so by boat around the island on which she stands, and so they will never see some of the finer details concerning the statue. One very significant thing, that perhaps goes unnoticed, even on pictures and photos of the statue, are the broken shackles and chains, at the feet of the woman, representing freedom from oppression and tyranny.

This made me think about that amazing account of the healing of the man in the land of the Gerasenes by Jesus- a man who was homeless, not in his right mind, naked and living an isolated life among the tombstones in the graveyard. He was fastened with shackles and chains but even broke free from these at times. What a horrible existence that must have been. *"This spirit had often taken control of the man. Even when he was placed under guard and put in chains and shackles, he simply broke them and rushed out into the wilderness, completely under the demon's power. Luke 8 v 29 NLT*

People were so frightened of him -his behaviour, appearance and his shackles and chains. Jesus went to the land of the Gerasenes to reach and to free just this one person. The transformation of the man was so complete that he was seen sitting at the feet of Jesus, fully clothed, perfectly sane, so that all who witnessed this were very afraid. His chains and shackles gone, and he was now free.

In Isaiah 58 verse 6 we read these beautiful words of liberation. *"Is not this the kind of fasting I have chosen: to loose the chains of injustice and untie the cords of the yoke, to set the oppressed free and break every yoke?*

PRAY for those who feel oppressed, trapped, held back, isolated, vulnerable, persecuted and set apart-that they might experience the liberation that Jesus longs to give to them. Pray also for justice, mercy, and freedom to be seen in the many areas of conflict that we hear of in our world.

There is a plaque at the foot of the statue contains a famous poem, by Emma Lazarus 1883, with these memorable words at the end the poem.

"Keep, ancient lands, your storied pomp!" cries she
With silent lips. "Give me your tired, your poor,
Your huddled masses yearning to breathe free,
The wretched refuse of your teeming shore.
Send these, the homeless, tempest-tossed to me,
I lift my lamp beside the golden door!"

Emma Lazarus 1883

Names at The Memorial Site

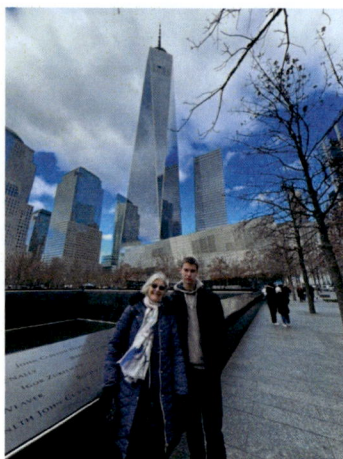

The 9/11 Memorial is a place of remembrance, honouring the 2,983 people killed in the terror attacks of September 11, 2001, and 1993. The site has two vast 1-acre (4,000 m²) man-made pools with waterfalls, set into the footprints of the former Twin Towers of the World Trade Centre. The waterfalls were intended to hide the sounds of the busy, noisy city, making the site a place of sanctuary. According to the architect, Michael Arad, the pools represent "absence made visible." Although water flows into the voids, the voids are never filled.

The names of those 2,983 people are inscribed into bronze ledges or parapets around the two memorial pools. Each person is clearly identified and never forgotten. This made me think about the importance of names, the family tree or genealogy of individuals.

We spend a lot of time choosing a name for a new son or daughter. Names have significant meanings, and sometimes they are established, significant family names. I spent a three-month period researching our family tree on the search engine Ancestry, which provided important historical information about one branch of the family. I hold the family archive in a filing cabinet, which contains not just the names and photographs of family members, but their historical documents, key letters, and artefacts. The children and grandchildren will one day ask-who are these people? Names, family trees, genealogies, ancestry searches are key to locating our place in time and history.

In fourteen books in the Bible there are long lists of names and lengthy genealogies. These names are the names of real people, with real histories, fixed in real time, in their family historical records. These lists of names, that we sometimes only scan over, demonstrate that God is concerned about each individual person in each family, mentioned by name. The genealogies demonstrate that God has been working through time towards an intended outcome, and that He seeks to use each person, no matter how unorthodox or perhaps imperfect they might be. In the genealogy of Jesus, we find the perhaps controversial and unorthodox individuals of Tamar, Rahab, Ruth, and Bathsheba.

God knows your name, your circumstances, and your family. Your name is written on His heart and on the palm of His hand. Your name is registered in heaven, and He is waiting to receive you there one day.

Some Bible verses to ponder:

But now the Lord who made you, O Jacob, and He who made you, O Israel, says, "Do not be afraid. For I have bought you and made you free. I have called you by name. You are Mine! Isaiah 43 v 1 NLV
When Jesus came by, he looked up at Zacchaeus and called him by name. "Zacchaeus!" he said. "Quick, come down! I must be a guest in your home today." Luke 19 v 5 NLT
See, I have written your name on the palms of my hands. Isaiah 49 v 16 NLT

But don't rejoice because evil spirits obey you; rejoice because your names are registered in heaven." Luke 10 v 20 NLT

Be like Children

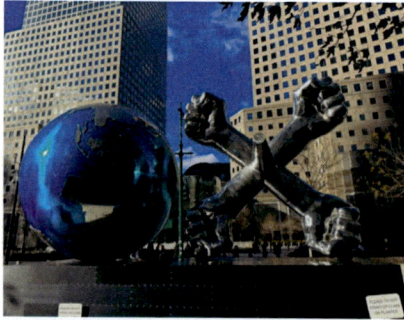

During the Lockdown days when we had limited access to outdoor spaces, we played a different game each day. We have a large selection of board games and worked through them all. The one game that we did not have was a simple game called Jacks. Jacks is played with small, shaped pieces called jacks, scattered into a small area, with a ball that the player tosses in the air. As the player tosses the ball, he quickly grabs the jacks before the ball bounces and lands. The aim is to gather as many jacks as possible before the ball lands. It is a game which dates to ancient times and is played by children worldwide.

The XO sculpture at the entrance to the new World Trade Centre, was inspired by this simple children's game. The X of the sculpture illustrates the jack with crossed arms each representing the four pillars of the XO World Project-equality, unity, peace, and love; and represents 'love' in sign language. The O represents a globe, intending to bring humanity together as one. Visitors are encouraged to take a selfie, with their arms crossed across their chest, in front of the XO and to post this on social media. The XO Project aims to inspire people worldwide to actively seek peace, and inclusion by engaging with the play principles of children, who seem to naturally welcome all races, ages, genders, religions, and nationalities. XO Play, a complementary sculpture, shows a group of children happily playing the game of jacks.

"My inspiration for these sculptures came from children and their open acceptance of others. A child's mind and heart are free of prejudice regardless of race, gender, or religion, which is how we should all strive to emulate." Daniel Anderson 2017

Jesus welcomed children. He wants each of us to be His little children-children of any age, six- to ninety-six-year-old children.

Then Jesus called for the children and said to the disciples, "Let the children come to me. Don't stop them! For the Kingdom of God belongs to those who are like these children. I tell you the truth, anyone who doesn't receive the Kingdom of God like a child will never enter it." Luke 18 v 5-6 NLT

Excerpts from I like Youngsters. From Prayers of Life by Michel Quoist

God says, I like youngsters. I want people to be like them.
I don't like old people unless they are still children. I want only children in my kingdom; this has been decreed from the beginning of time.
Youngsters—twisted, humped, wrinkled, white-bearded—all kinds of youngsters, but youngsters.
There is no changing it; it has been decided, there is room for no one else.
I like little children because my likeness has not yet been dulled in them. They have not botched my likeness. They are new, pure without a blot, without a smear.
So, when I gently lean over them, I recognize myself in them.
Open, all of you, little old men!
It is I, your God, the eternal, risen from the dead, coming to bring back to life the child in you.

But to all who believed him and accepted him, he gave the right to become children of God. They are reborn—not with a physical birth resulting from human passion or plan, but a birth that comes from God. John 1 v 12-13 NLT
See how very much our Father loves us, for he calls us his children, and that is what we are! But the people who belong to this world don't recognize that we are God's children because they don't know him. Dear friends, we are already God's children, but he has not yet shown us what we will be like when Christ appears. 1 John 3 v 1-2 NLT.

The C Journey

Interruptions - Stepping out of the busy

My cancer journey has caused a significant interruption to my diary, my weeks, my sleep pattern, my energy levels, my family and social life, my involvement in things, and clearly my health. It is an unwelcome but necessary interruption. But it is not comfortable. So, when major interruptions happen you can resist and complain, or you can go with it and use the experience to see what lessons it may hold for you. I am a naturally busy, active person and so to have to put a large chunk of things to one side is a challenge and frustrating. I resist the need to slow down, to give things up, and to stop. There is always the 'tyranny of the urgent', the things that must be done, now and not later. So, how I am making the change and the adjustments? Perhaps not very well if truth be told.

In the familiar story of the good Samaritan, told by the Master Storyteller Himself, the Samaritan faced a dramatic interruption. All the other characters in the story had something important to do, somewhere to be, somewhere to go, a function, a role, a significant focus and they did not desire to be interrupted. By contrast, the Samaritan suspended his plans, his important journey, his focus, the tasks that he had to perform, to attend to, the urgent need in front of him. He was willing to be interrupted. It cost him time, effort, thought, care, money, and disrupted his present and possibly his future schedule, as he would need to return that way. Yet, he stopped. He stepped out of the busy.

Then a despised Samaritan came along, and when he saw the man, he felt compassion for him. Going over to him, the Samaritan soothed his wounds with olive oil and wine and bandaged them. Then he put the man on his own donkey and took him to an inn, where he took care of him. The next day he handed the innkeeper two silver coins, telling him, 'Take care of this man. If his bill runs higher than this, I'll pay you the next time I'm here.'
Luke 10v 33-35 NLT

There will always be interruptions. How will we use them? How can we turn them into positives? There is a familiar phrase that 'we always have time to do what God would have us do'. I came across this thought by David Kossoff, the son of Jewish Russian immigrants, and so I add it here.

Lord, teach me how to stand still.
To switch off; to lean on a gate; to sit and look at your beautiful world.
Teach me how to leave the phone off,
to slacken speed, to lie in the sun without
a feeling that I should be doing something.
Teach me Lord, to stop, to stop fussing,
to stop working at it, to stop keeping on bravely,
to stop doing it all myself (no help you know, all by myself).
Teach me Lord, to let others help me.
Teach me to delegate, to trust.
That which I do, let's face it, is not so important.
Doing it alone makes me feel it is important.
It also makes me feel tired and irritable and anxious and fearful
of what will happen if I'm off sick.
and not liking the thought that very little
would happen, that the earth would not shake
and probably nobody would notice for a week or two.
Why can't I stop running, Lord?
Teach me Lord, to stop, to look, and listen.
To be still in the mind when I stop.
To see beauty when I look.
To hear more when I listen.
David Kossoff from You have a Minute Lord?

Empty and Full

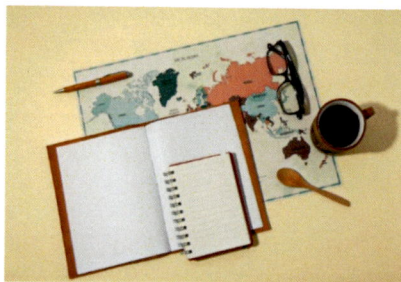

Father, may I live this day to the full.

When we were both working full time with four young children and both sets of aging parents living nearby, my daily and weekly diary was very full. It had appointments for the children, school events and holidays, parents' evenings and staff meetings, swimming lessons, evening Uniformed Organisations, medical and dental appointments, church events and all sorts of extraneous events to fix in the planner. Life was busy and full. As the children were growing up and moving on then holiday and university visits were added into the planners. One of my busiest periods of time was perhaps the pandemic period when visiting many of our elderly church folk became extremely important. Those busy periods of time seem a long time ago now.

These days, my weekly diary looks rather empty. There are some fixed appointments, but now I no longer need that daily check on the diary to see what my day or week will hold- visits, church sessions, shopping trips. The diary has gone from almost full to empty. In many ways our human preference is for these busy daily and weekly markers that perhaps make us feel useful, significant, and essential. These markers and events are important to us and many of us keep our old diaries going way back in time.

Yet, I am beginning to learn that every day, -whether empty or full- is a gift from God. Each new day is the day that the Lord has made, to rejoice and be glad in. Psalm 118 v 24. Jesus is present with us in each new day- empty or full. His presence, grace and favour meet us in that day. So, whether your diary is choc a block full, or your week is stretching out in front of you with a rather empty feel and lots of 'blank' days, may we be thankful for what God is continuing to do for us and with us in each new day. That new day is a gift from God, and whatever that day holds, is known to God and can be used by Him and us, with thankful hearts. God will meet with us in each new day, -every day.

The Lectio 365 daily prayer begins with these words: Father, may I live this day to the full, being true to you in every way. We can give thanks today to our faithful God and He can use us in this day as He can use us at no other time. He has kept us in the past and He waits for us in the days ahead and our unknown future. We receive from His fulness grace upon grace upon grace, a grace that is continuous, inexhaustible, and limitless. May our today be full of His grace and presence.

And of his fullness have all we received, and grace for grace John 1 v 16 GNT;   May you experience the love of Christ, though it is too great to understand fully. Then you will be made complete with all the fullness of life and power that comes from God. Ephesians 3 v 19 NLT

Lectio 365 Prayer
Father, may I live this day to the full, being true to you in every way.
Jesus, help me to give myself away to others, being kind to everyone I meet.
Spirit, help me to love the lost, proclaiming Christ in all I say and do.
Amen.

Grace in the place-the place of testing

Unanticipated trials and challenges are generally not welcomed. We may hope that we will somehow be saved and protected from these kinds of things and yet often this is not the case, and the road in front of us may suddenly become difficult, discouraging, beyond our understanding, and perhaps also beyond our usual coping mechanisms. Yet we try to keep walking in trust along with our faithful God. It would be easy to harbour negative thoughts, to complain, go into avoidance mode, or even begin to doubt our trust and confidence in the God who loves us. But on this kind of journey, we need to know and to depend on the God who will be there with us. We need to know that in that time of hard testing, He will keep us safe. Can we trust that He will give us the resources and strength for whatever we need on any testing journey?

Every test that you have experienced is the kind that normally comes to people. But God keeps his promise, and He will not allow you to be tested beyond your power to remain firm; at the time you are put to the test, he will give you the strength to endure it, and so provide you with a way out. 1 Corinthians 10 v 13 GNT

In the Lord's Prayer, Jesus modelled a prayer marked by a relationship and a trust in His Father. We may pray for protection against the ills, trials, tests and challenges of life in our own lives and that of our families, but there is no guarantee of this for us. What He does promise to us is to keep us safe and to walk with us though the experience and the trial.

Do not bring us to hard testing but keep us safe from the Evil One. Matthew 6 v 13 GNT

I have learned from experience that it can be helpful to prepare for the unexpected, the twists and turns in life, the shocks and the shadows. This is not to be gloomy or fearful of the tests and trials that may come, but not to be shocked by them. Anticipation and preparation are two significant things that we can build on. So, how may we prepare ourselves for the bumps in the road? For they will surely come at some point. They are the kinds of tests that' normally come.' We need to safeguard and grow that close relationship with the Father, trust His faithfulness, and grace and curb that desire to rely on our own strength and ability.

I have just watched Sunday's Songs of Praise, and the closing hymn was the beautiful hymn written by George Matheson. The hymn assures us that

Love will not let us go, that he will seek us through the pain and trials, and that there will be a rainbow after rain.

O Love, that wilt not let me go,
I rest my weary soul in Thee;
I give Thee back the life I owe,
That in Thine ocean depths its flow
May richer, fuller be.

O Joy, that seekest me through pain,
I cannot close my heart to Thee;
I trace the rainbow through the rain,
And feel the promise is not vain
That morn shall tearless be.

PRAY
I am safe in the deep waters, the shallows, the turbulent, crashing waves, because you are holding me. Help me to trust you.

Patience

designed by freepik

Consider it a sheer gift, friends, when tests and challenges come at you from all sides. You know that under pressure, your faith-life is forced into the open and shows its true colours. So don't try to get out of anything prematurely. Let it do its work, so you become mature and well-developed, not deficient in any way. James 1 v 4 MSG

I thought that I was good at patience! I am by nature even tempered, calm, deliberate and controlled. I hoped that my patience was a mixture of basic temperament and years of experience. But every so often testing circumstances crop up that indicates that I am not nearly as far along the scale of patience as I thought I was. As I entered for my appointment yesterday the sign said that there was a waiting time of one and a half hours, which then became two hours and finally two and a half hours. "Please take a seat in the waiting area." Three hours later they were ready for action.

We have grown used to things being instantly provided, fast, quick results and resolutions. We are often in a hurry and become impatient with delays. We become impatient with systems, individuals, family members, partners, let alone those 'sandpaper' people who have a knack of rubbing us up the wrong way. I know that 'my times are in God's hands' and that He plans and orders for my good, but the practicalities can be a frustration.

So, the way forward in times like this? I need a bit of 'self-talk as well as 'God talk. 'I need to clear my thoughts and organise my feelings. A good bit of logic and rationality does not go amiss. I need to be calm and focussed and look at any situation 'in the whole.' I need to consider what I am not able to change and look at what I might be able to change. Calmness and restraint are helpful as well as putting yourself in the other person's shoes or circumstances. And can I turn each situation into thankfulness and praise?

Since God chose you to be the holy people he loves, you must clothe yourselves with tender-hearted mercy, kindness, humility, gentleness, and patience. Colossians 3 v 12 NLT

But the Holy Spirit produces this kind of fruit in our lives: love, joy, peace, patience, kindness, goodness, faithfulness, gentleness, and self-control. There is no law against these things! Galatians 5 v 22-23 NLT

Fill now my life, O Lord my God, in every part with praise:
that my whole being may proclaim your being and your ways.
Not for the lip of praise alone, nor yet the praising heart,
I ask, but for a life made up of praise in every part:

Praise in the common things of life, its goings out and in;
praise in each duty and each deed, exalted or unseen.
Fill every part of me with praise let all my being speak
of you and of your love, O Lord, poor though I be and weak.

Horatius Bonar

PRAY I need patience and gentleness when the going gets tough. I need kindness in my voice, my manner, my body language when I feel impatient, frustrated, and downhearted. Help me to turn things into praise.

Dealing with Uncertainty

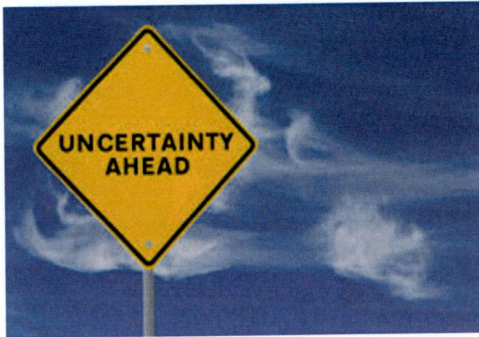

Trust God from the bottom of your heart; don't try to figure out everything on your own. Listen for God's voice in everything you do, everywhere you go; He's the one who will keep you on track. Don't assume that you know it all. Run to God! Proverbs 3 v 6 MSG

In all your ways know, recognize, and acknowledge Him, and He will direct and make straight and plain your paths. Proverbs 3 v 6 AMP

I like predictability and control and yet this week I faced a situation where things became unpredictable, precarious and uncertain and it was an uncomfortable situation to be in. I am a planner and an ace preparer, which I must admit gives me that sense of control over things that I very much need, to feel comfortable and to eliminate confusion and concern. I like clarity, and certainty. I guess that I am a bit of a 'control freak.'

So, this week, I hit a bump in the road which could have knocked me off course and delayed my journey. When you are not able to see clearly the road ahead, when an outcome is not guaranteed, or there are several outcomes that are confusing and contradictory, then this kind of uncertainty and conflict can be de stabilising.

I realized that I was not dealing with the uncertainty in an appropriate way. As a Christian, where was the trust and dependence on God in this situation? There was a need to challenge my need for certainty, to accept the uncertainty, and to trust Him with it. How have I overcome such situations before and how has assurance and confidence been restored? I needed to consider how I have restored the balance before and seek God's face and wisdom to get back on the road of trust. I needed to give myself a good talking to! What is the way forward? -Talk to the Father. Tell Him what is on your mind and heart. Tell Him about your frustration and even share your anger, dismay, and confusion. Get real with God. Pass it back to Him. Reflect on times in the past when you may have been in this situation and come through it. Then step aside for a while, look after yourself and do something that supports self-care. Share your journey and problem with a friend. Support is always there.

May the God of hope fill you with all joy and peace as you trust in Him, so that you may overflow with hope by the power of the Holy Spirit. Romans 15 v 13 NIV

PRAY
Father, we pray for those who are confused, and in a position of doubt and uncertainty.

We pray for those whose outcome has not turned out as expected.

We pray for those where the outlook may seem to be temporarily uncertain.

May they hold on to your peace and your presence. Walk with them on this uncertain road.

Patience and endurance in the long haul

We also pray that you will be strengthened with all His glorious power so you will have all the endurance and patience you need. May you be filled with joy. Colossians 1 v 11 NLT

Sometimes in life, the challenges that come are sudden, unexpected, urgent but may be short lived, so that the steep mountain of stress, discomfort and dismay, although unbearably and painfully challenging, is conquered, and life is able to move on at a pace again. But sometimes the challenge is not a sharp Himalayan climb but a long-drawn-out trek across an indistinguishable, barren route with few landmarks to guide, reassure and to measure progress. The road just goes on indefinitely into the future and it is hard to fix your eyes on that final victory. That kind of challenge needs an extra grace to keep going for the long haul.

There are many folks who are in this position who need the daily grit, energy, and patience to get up and get going, knowing that there will be many, many more days like this one. They need that patient endurance and stickability that Paul speaks of here. Even the most resourceful and strong need the power of our most glorious God to remain focussed and faith filled. This kind of stamina and strength cannot be worked up from nowhere. God provides it in abundance- and with joy as an added measure. He will provide the inner strength for the long haul.

It is comforting too to be accompanied on the journey by those who will walk parts of the road with you, lifting your spirits, encouraging, sharing and supporting in a myriad of ways, that may seem small to them, but which have the gift to move your steps forward. Be thankful for those companions and fellow hikers on the journey.

We are praying, too, that you will be filled with his mighty, glorious strength so that you can keep going no matter what happens—always full of the joy of the Lord, TLB

We pray that you'll have the strength to stick it out over the long haul— not the grim strength of gritting your teeth but the glory-strength God gives. It is strength that endures the unendurable and spills over into joy, thanking the Father who makes us strong enough to take part in everything bright and beautiful that he has for us. MSG

Even to your old age and grey hairs
I am He; I am He who will sustain you.
I have made you and I will carry you;
I will sustain you and I will rescue you.   Isaiah 46 v 4

PRAY   You are a personal God, always present, always providing and your purposes are true and faithful.

Stories that connect us - Vulnerability

When we share our stories, our concerns, our joys, our triumphs, and experiences, these can connect us to others. We share our experience, and it opens a door for the other to share their story. We speak and then we listen. It is a good thing to share. We are all storytellers with something to share. I recently came across this poem, Vulnerability, by John Roedel which captures the art of storytelling and connection.

Vulnerability doesn't mean telling others what happened to us from across a café table or from behind a microphone. And then going home from the experience feeling just as alone as you did before. Vulnerability means allowing your human heart blanket to get sewn to other heart blankets.

It's about connection.
We don't do it for status
We do it for synergy
We don't confess for clout
We do it to build community.
We tell our tale
to invite others
to tell theirs.

It's the sacred cycle
Of storytelling.
We gather in a circle of trust and
Say "here is my journey."
Then we listen to
The other journeys
That are shared
We take space
then we give space

We pour
Then we absorb
We speak
Then we listen
We are storytellers
Then we are witnesses

Vulnerability isn't just about
Grave digging in our past
To expose our skeletons
It's about sewing quilts

Here is my patch
Here is your patch
Here is their patch
here is our story
John "patchwork heart" Roedel

Scars

I would guess that most of us have a scar or two, either caused by a fall, an accident or injury, or surgery of some kind, either big or small, or maybe even a small burn. The healing processes of our bodies are truly wonderful. When skin is injured or cut in some way, new tissue is created which helps the skin to reseal itself. The scar helps the skin to repair its damaged tissue, to close the gap made by a cut, tear or surgical incision, and pulls together the wound. Isn't that amazing! Our skin is such an essential part of our immune system. I am the proud bearer of several scars and surgical incisions. My first scar was caused when I was 10 years old and collided with a run of iron railings. The second scar followed the safe, emergency delivery of our first child. The third scar was to remove a facial blemish, and the fourth, more major scar, was the removal of a cancer. So, I have had my share of surgical scars. Such scars may fade over time but often remain.

There are also hidden scars that may be hidden, hard to detect, or deliberately concealed. People may carry emotional scars caused by distress of some nature. There may be a loss, a breakdown of a relationship, a mental health concern, the responsibility for the care of an aged partner or parent, a long-term health condition, and a whole range of other circumstances. A person may carry these burdens alone and those folk around them may not recognise the hidden trauma and scarring that is caused. Such scars may take a long time to heal and fade.

We have a Saviour who seeks to heal and to restore. A healing of any wound is a first essential, but Jesus is in the business of recovery, renewal, and restoration. Then He said to the man, "Stretch out your hand." So, he stretched it out and it was completely restored, just as sound as the other. Matthew 12 v 13 NIV

Then he showed me the river of the water of life, sparkling like crystal as it flowed from the throne of God and of the Lamb. In the middle of the street of the city and on either bank of the river grew the tree of life, bearing twelve fruits, a different kind for each month. The leaves of the tree were for the healing of the nations. Revelation 22 v 1-2 JBP

Recently, our thoughts have been with those who have said goodbye to long time partners and other dear family members. I came across this song Scars in Heaven, by Casting Crowns. It is a strong reminder that there will be no scars in heaven, other than those scars on the body, feet and hands of our Lord. We will be renewed and fully restored.

SONG

The only scars in Heaven, they won't belong to me and you
There'll be no such thing as broken, and all the old will be made new
And the thought that makes me smile now, even as the tears fall down
Is that the only scars in Heaven are on the hands that hold you now

Songwriters: John Mark Hall / Matthew Joseph West

Scars in Heaven lyrics © O/B/O DistroKid, Sony/ATV Music Publishing LLC

https://www.youtube.com/watch?v=BCc7TCmKcwQ

PRAY for those grieving the loss of loved ones, experiencing physical or emotional scars. May we be sensitive to their situation and kind in our words.

And the God of all grace, who called you to his eternal glory in Christ, after you have suffered a little while, will Himself restore you and make you strong, firm and steadfast. To Him be the power for ever and ever. Amen. 1 Peter 5 v 10-11 NIV

Trust-in the Fog

As I was driving back in the car late-into the evening, the night was bleak, dark and foreboding, and the nighttime sky was heavy with rain, black clouds, and thick gloom. It was difficult to see where the edges of the road were. Our main country road has no street lighting or pavements at either side, but simple grass verges-with major holes, dips and a small beck at the edge. It reminded me of a time, when as a younger, more inexperienced driver, I was driving in deep fog. It was difficult to see even two metres in front of the car and even after trying to follow the white edges of the pavement, I found myself not on the road at all, but on the forecourt of a parade of shops. I judged it wise to stop and get out of the car.

There are times in life when we are in a place of confusion, disappointment, lacking clarity and a clear focus for the way ahead. It can be distressing 'not to know' the way ahead, not to be sure of the outcome, and not to know if the desired result or answer to a prayer will be realized. There is a risk of going off the road and on to the forecourt where we are stuck for a while, or of trying to manufacture our own solution to a desired result.

Many will be familiar with my C journey. The very worst part of that journey was the five months of chemotherapy with its unpleasant and disabling side effects. Initially, the powerful drugs seemed to be effective but then during the second round of chemo an MRI scan clearly showed that the tumour had doubled in size and that the move to surgery was essential. The surgical team were superb, and the final pathology report and further MRIs confirmed that there was no spread of the cancer. So, although that news was excellent, I was still left confused, and saddened, that after the five months of treatment with its significant delay to resolution, those months seemed to be wasted, bleak and fog bound. But with God nothing is wasted, there are always lessons to be learned. I had trusted Him.

It is in those times of weakness and disorientation that you need the prayer support of others. Prayer needs energy, patience and vision. There are times when you have none of those. At those times of confusion, we need to trust a loving God and surrender to His outcome. I was so glad of the prayer support of our Leaders, the Sunday prayer team, the church prayer link, the church fellowship, friends around the country and abroad, and anyone who prayed at that time. On the day of the surgery, the presence of Jesus was tangible. It was so evident that He was with me.

So, when we are in the fog, don't keep pushing ahead. It is safer to stop and reach out to friends for prayer and help.

Don't fret or worry. Instead of worrying, pray. Let petitions and praises shape your worries into prayers, letting God know your concerns. Before you know it, a sense of God's wholeness, everything coming together for good, will come and settle you down. It's wonderful what happens when Christ displaces worry at the centre of your life. Philippians 4 v 6 MSG

PRAY
Have I trials and temptations?
Is there trouble anywhere?
I should never be discouraged;
Take it to the Lord in prayer.

Can I find a friend so faithful,
Who will all my sorrows share?
Jesus knows my every weakness;
Take it to the Lord in prayer.

Am I weak and heavy laden,
Cumbered with a load of care?
Precious Savior, still my refuge!
Take it to the Lord in prayer.

Adapted from words by Joseph Medlicott Scriven

Encourage one another

Therefore encourage one another and build each other up, just as in fact you are doing. 1 Thessalonians 5 v 11 NIV

Finally, brothers and sisters, rejoice! Strive for full restoration, encourage one another, be of one mind, live in peace. And the God of love and peace will be with you. 2 Corinthians 13 v 11 NIV

During this past week I have received some wonderful, practical encouragements which have spurred me on, in what could have been a very challenging week. Paul, in the verses from Thessalonians, challenged the early Christians to strengthen, encourage, and build each other up in every way and not just in their faith in Christ. Paul knew the importance of connection and the need to spur each person on, to give support, hope, encouragement and confidence to fellow Christian family members. We all need a good dose of encouragement from time to time and not just when we are going through a challenging or a dark patch. That text message, email, card, letter, batch of buns, flowers, surprise treat or whatever it may be, is just the thing that may lift the spirits and spur somebody on at just the right moment. It may be a small, or a costly thing for the giver, but the mutual joy and encouragement that follows for both giver and receiver can be significant. The giver turns their eyes from their situation, busyness and circumstances, to consider in love, the needs of another. The recipient delights at an unexpected gift, text or card which is a tangible boost to their confidence and a massive encouragement.

Paul, in this very practical letter, goes on to ask those early Christians to consider especially, those who have responsibilities for them, who guide and lead them in their church fellowships. We are also to recognize and appreciate our leaders and supporters for who they are, to value, and acknowledge them. These folk need some practical encouragement as well. In this way, by living in peace, love and encouragement we will build each other up.

May the God who inspires men to endure, and gives them a Father's care, give you a mind united towards one another because of your common loyalty to Jesus Christ. And then, as one man, you will sing from the heart the praises of God the Father of our Lord Jesus Christ. So, open your hearts to one another as Christ has opened his heart to you, and God will be glorified. Romans 15 v5-7 JBP

PRAY
Father, help us to open our hearts to each other.

Help us to find opportunities to encourage others.

May we especially think about our church leaders, leadership team, and all our volunteer leaders who give their service so willingly to others. May no-one go unnoticed. May we be encouragers.

Family, Family and Family

We are very privileged to belong to several families. We have our own nuclear family, our son and daughters, grandchildren, aunts and uncles, and several distant relatives. We love them dearly and keep in regular contact as much as possible, even though distance from Leeds can present challenges.

We also have our church family at MBC which has become a very significant part of our lives, and particularly very recently. Our Christian family at MBC has begun to feel like a real family. We have felt a deep 'ground swell' of love developing in our fellowship, which has become almost tangible. One of our newer members calls me 'sister.' There is a sense of a shared awareness of the needs within the congregation and a willingness to respond to those needs practically, prayerfully, with numerous methods of contact, and connection. There is a deep change that has been happening.

Then we have our China family. For many, many years we have had connections with key Research colleagues, men and women who are Leaders and senior members of several top Universities and Institutions, in Sichuan, Beijing, and Changchun. Through many years of regular contact, communication, support, visits to China, research exchange visits to Bradford and China, and their visits to our home, we have established a close connection- a family connection. We are regarded as family members, and we know many of them as family. When the news of my illness and surgery was shared with them, they immediately responded with messages of love, concern and even prayers. "Jane is a very important member of our AMRI family, and we are always with you." When Phil returned from his most recent trip to China, he brought back with him a bag of Chinese medicine and many other personal gifts - tangible demonstrations of their love.

Over many years we have connected with some wonderful Christian individuals and families and have become involved with them, their challenges, successes, work and witness. It is a joy and a challenge to know so many people and to stay in connection. Family is about connection-real connection. I am so thankful that I am a part of these different families.

So then, as often as we have the chance, we should do good to everyone, and especially to those who belong to our family in the faith. Galatians 6 v 10 GNT

A nighttime prayer.
The peace of God be over me to shelter me.
Under me to uphold me.

About me to protect me.
Behind me to direct me
Ever with me to save me.
The peace of all peace be mine this night
In the name of the Father, Son, and Holy Spirit.

Give thanks

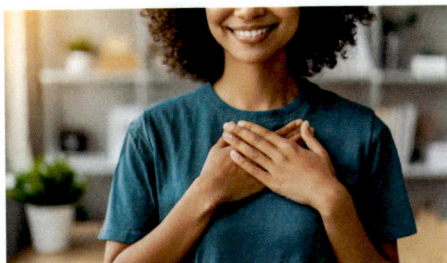

*In every situation, no matter what the circumstances, be
thankful and continually give thanks to God; for this is the will of God for
you in Christ Jesus.* 1 Thessalonians 5 v 18 AMP

This week I attended a women's worship evening joining with over 300
other women of different ages and backgrounds as we worshipped
together. As we praised, prayed and sang our worship songs, one chorus
really encouraged me and lifted my heart and soul. It was an old chorus
from way back- 'give thanks with a grateful heart.' It was good to be
reminded that even though the worship hall was full of women, each
individual unique, each with their own concerns, prayers of thanks- the
Father listens to each voice-He hears your one voice in the crowd. You
are not one among the many, concealed in the multitude, your voice and
your needs and your praise hidden and merged. He is tuned into you
and your voice. Knowing the Father heart of God, we can give thanks,
confidently bringing every situation, and every circumstance to Him and
praising Him for that time, that place, that situation, and that
circumstance. Because of what Jesus has done for us. He will bring glory
to His name.

Give thanks with a grateful heart
Give thanks to the Holy One
Give thanks because He's given Jesus Christ, His Son

And now let the weak say, "I am strong"
Let the poor say, "I am rich
Because of what the Lord has done for us"

Rejoice always, pray continually, give thanks in all circumstances; for this is God's will for you in Christ Jesus. 1 Thessalonians 5 v 16-18

Make thankfulness your sacrifice to God, and keep the vows you made to the Most High.   Then call on me when you are in trouble, and I will rescue you, and you will give me glory. Psalm 50 v 14-15 NLT

Sadness, and a change of perception

Today, Friday, is a sad day personally, as it is the funeral of a very good High School friend of longstanding. Her husband was the best man at our wedding. We were nurtured as young Christians in the same church and had many happy days and challenges together. So today is a time of remembering those happy memories of school days, of post exam days, of catching up days and holidays, of shared meals, and life events, of looking back at photographs, and sharing the struggles of illness and final days.

Today, her partner of many years, will release her and see her go into safer hands. For all of us it is a change of perception. We let her go and say goodbye for now, as she goes to her destined port, where other voices welcome her home, and she is free in the welcome of her Saviour.

I am standing upon the seashore. A ship, at my side,
spreads her white sails to the moving breeze and starts
for the blue ocean. She is an object of beauty and strength.
I stand and watch her until, at length, she hangs like a speck
of white cloud just where the sea and sky come to mingle with each
other.

Then, someone at my side says, "There, she is gone."

Gone where?

Gone from my sight. That is all. She is just as large in mast,
hull and spar as she was when she left my side.
And, she is just as able to bear her load of living freight to her destined
port.
Her diminished size is in me — not in her.

And, just at the moment when someone says, "There, she is gone,"
there are other eyes watching her coming, and other voices
ready to take up the glad shout, "Here she comes!"

And that is dying…

By Rev. Luther F. Beecher (1813-1903)

He will wipe away all tears from their eyes, and there shall be no more
death, nor sorrow, nor crying, nor pain. All of that has gone forever.
Revelation 21v 4 NLT

PRAY for those who have said goodbye to loved ones. May their memories be full and joyous and bring peace of mind and soul.

The steadfast love of the Lord never ceases

I have recently written the following verses from Lamentations into a birthday card and then a couple of days later, a wonderful Christian friend sent these same words to me, with a reminder also of the old, familiar chorus.

The faithful love of the Lord never ends.
His mercies never cease.
Great is his faithfulness;
His mercies begin afresh each morning.
I say to myself, "The Lord is my inheritance;
therefore, I will hope in Him!"

The Lord is good to those who depend on him,
to those who search for Him.
So it is good to wait quietly
for salvation from the Lord.
Lamentations 3 v 22-26 NLT

Chorus

The steadfast love of the Lord never ceases.
His mercies never come to an end.
They are new every morning, new every morning
Great is your faithfulness Oh Lord.
Great is your faithfulness.

The Book of Lamentations, written by Jeremiah, is a 'lament,' an outpouring of sorrow and loss, the reality of pain and tragedy. It primarily focuses on the losses Israel caused by turning away from God. It is bleak. But then Jeremiah realises that he has hope and an expectation of God's mercy and love. He looks to God's faithfulness, HThat turning point propels him forward to a more positive stance where he can see from experience in the past, the God who is merciful, faithful, and whose tender mercies are fresh every day.

At the very end of Lamentations are the following words. This is the language of hope.

Turn us to Yourself, O Lord, and we shall be turned and restored! Renew our days as of old!   Lamentations 5 v 21

So, these very familiar, well-loved verses, are for those who perhaps feel to be in a challenging situation. There are those we know who have lost loved ones, those who have health concerns, those who feel isolated and without support, and there are others perhaps whose pain and discomfort is silent and unknown. Let us ask our faithful God to turn our eyes and our focus to Him. Then we will be turned, see, and be renewed to know God's tender mercies which are new every morning.

The Cancer Journey for Children and Teenagers

The Cancer journey for anyone is particularly tough and can be lengthy. But I have become aware of how challenging this same journey is for small children, young people, and their families. Many family things, careers, jobs, must be 'put on hold' while the focus is placed on the child with cancer.

At the hospital today, my eyes were drawn to a new poster in the reception area. It introduced you to a young child who has Ewing Sarcoma, which is a rare type of bone cancer. He was diagnosed with this cancer when he was six years of age. Initially, he required 14 cycles of chemotherapy which was given over ten months, which was then followed by radiotherapy.

His mum says "the chemotherapy was horrific. He had 14 cycles with a 2-week gap between each cycle, but his body took so long to recover, that in total it took around ten months. Besides being extremely tough on our son it was difficult for the whole family. I had three children then, and I now have four, and it was hard for our other children not to lose their parents completely. We took it in turns each night as we didn't have childcare."

"The treatment is brutal, and the chance of relapse is terrifying. We have to do something. We need to pull some good out of everything we went through."

Now 11 years of age, he now faces long term side effects including thyroid and growth hormone problems, and he relies on emergency cortisone injections to help his body recover from any shocks."

The words of this loving mum and the journey of this young man really impacted me. I have a phrase that I read in a motivational book some years ago that keeps coming back to me. You can 'forge meaning' out of any difficult situation or trial that you are forced to endure. We can turn things around for good, for ourselves, and for other people. Our experience may help others who are facing what seem to be insurmountable challenges.

Pray
For families with young children who are navigating the cancer journey. For the siblings who may feel overlooked. That they may all have times of relief, fun, joy, and peace in the middle of the turmoil.

Fresh light on the familiar Psalms

Psalm 23

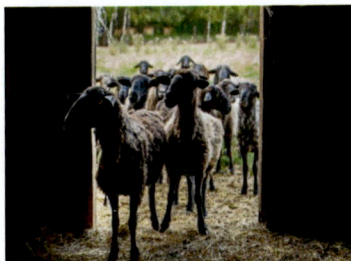

Whatever this new week may hold for you in terms of busyness, activity, or work, it is good to return to this familiar psalm of David and to be refreshed, refocussed, and renewed. So, I commend this lovely version of Psalm 23 to you.

The 23rd Psalm for busy people:
The Lord is my pace setter. I shall not rush.
He makes me stop and rest for quiet intervals.
He provides me with images of stillness which restore my serenity.
He leads me in ways of efficiency through calmness of mind,
and His guidance is peace.
Even though I have a great many things to accomplish each day,
I will not fret for His presence is here.
His timelessness, His all importance, will keep me in balance.
He prepares refreshment and renewal in the midst of my activity,
by anointing my mind with his oils of tranquillity.
My cup of joyous energy overflows.
Surely harmony and effectiveness shall be the fruits of my hours.
For I shall walk at the pace of my Lord and dwell in His house forever.

Tobi Miyashina of Japan.

Psalm 32

I will instruct thee and teach thee in the way which thou shalt go. I will guide thee with mine eye. **Psalm 32 v 8 KJV**

Psalm 32, a contemplation, or meditation, written by David, is a psalm focussing on God's forgiveness, protection, and gracious leading. This verse offers a wonderful promise, that as a follower of Jesus, I have memorized and hung on to. God promises to guide us with His eye. He wants us to stay so close to Him that we can clearly know and see the correct path in front of us. It is true that 'His eye is on us', and we are always in His sight, but the verse has the sense that He will guide us 'with His eye'. Our focus should be so firmly on Him, looking to Him, so that we are sensitive and responsive to His leading. David says that we are not to be like the horse or mule who are turned only with difficulty using bit and bridle. Some horses also need the additional support of eye blinkers to direct their gaze forward. We are to' check in' with Jesus frequently, catch His eye, and wait for His nod of request or approval. God wants to take us into new and exciting places- places that we have not been to before. What a lovely thought.

The Passion Translation of the Psalm puts it like this.

I hear the Lord saying, "I will stay close to you, instructing and guiding you along the pathway for your life. I will advise you along the way and lead you forth with my eyes as your guide. So, don't make it difficult, don't be stubborn when I take you where you've not been before. Don't make me tug you and pull you along. Just come with me! TPT

PRAY
Help us to keep catching your eye. To keep checking in with you. Life runs so fast and so help us to slow down, wait and see what things you have for us.

Some words from a very old hymn:
All the way my Savior leads me
What have I to ask beside?
Can I doubt His faithful mercies?
Who through life has been my guide
Heavenly peace, divinest comfort
Ere by faith in Him to dwell
For I know whate'er befall me
Jesus doeth all things well

Taste and see: Psalm 34

Phil and I have attended many Chinese banquets over the years where the vast array of foods and flavours are presented to guests in the centre of the table. Chinese colleagues urge you to "try this", "taste this", and even place samples of the food on to your dish for you. I have been offered and encouraged to taste, frogs, snakes, eel, dog meat, cow heel, chicken feet, donkey soup, sheep's eyes and other bizarre and unfamiliar items that are strange and foreign to our western diet and palate. Yet I had to taste and see for myself, sometimes surreptitiously removing the food from my mouth and placing it into a napkin to be discarded at some opportune time. But I had to taste, sample, and discern for myself what was right for me personally to keep and consume. Chinese colleagues could recommend, but my choice had to be personal.

In these beautiful, memorable words from David, he encourages us to taste for ourselves the goodness of God, assuring us that we will have everything that we need for our lives.

O taste and see that the Lord is good: blessed is the man that trusteth in him. O fear the Lord, ye his saints: for there is no want to them that fear him. The young lions do lack and suffer hunger: but they that seek the Lord shall not want any good thing. Psalm 34 v 9-10 KJV

Open your mouth and taste, open your eyes, and see how good God is. Blessed are you who run to him. Worship God if you want the best. Worship opens doors to all his goodness.Young lions on the prowl get hungry, but God-seekers are full of God. MSG

David was a fugitive, running from Saul and then escaping his capture by the Philistines. This was perhaps one of the lowest points of his life and yet in this psalm he is filled with praise, worship, and trust for his lord. David encouraged his band of followers, and us, to taste, see and experience this loving, saving God for themselves. Each one must have a personal experience of God. It cannot be second hand.

A new song for a new day: Psalm 40

Psalm 40, a psalm of worship and thanks, was addressed 'to David's Chief Musician'. He only wanted the best musicians and voices to sing this song of praise with him! David had endured immense hardships, but he had come through. He had 'waited patiently for the Lord' and the Lord had 'leaned over' to listen to him. So now, David had a new song to sing. He wanted everyone to know what God had done.

And he hath put a new song in my mouth, even praise unto our God: many shall see it and fear and shall trust in the Lord. Psalm 40 v 3 KJV

I love the Passion Translation of this same verse: *A new song for a new day rises up in me every time I think about how He breaks through for me. Ecstatic praise pours out of my mouth until everyone hears how God has set me free. Many will see His miracles. They'll stand in awe of God and fall in love with Him. Blessing after blessing comes to those who love and trust the Lord.* TPT

We too can have a new song for each new day. Let's start by thanking Him for something small-a little blessing! May we be thankful for His kindness, love, and blessings to us each new day and speak it out to others.

Let the Spirit stimulate your souls. Express your joy in singing among yourselves psalms and hymns and spiritual songs, making music in your hearts for the ears of God! Thank God at all times for everything, in the name of our Lord Jesus Christ. Ephesians 5 v 19 JBP

PRAY
For those who are struggling today that God will 'come through for them' today. Give them a song of joy-a new song.

Fruit or Frustration Psalm 127

Except the Lord build the house, they labour in vain that build it: Except the Lord keep the city, the watchman waketh but in vain. Psalm 127 v 1 KJV

We have some experience of building. Some years ago, we owned a standard 3-bedroom detached house which sat on a large corner plot. We had architects' plans drawn up to double the size of the house into a 6 bedroomed house with extended living space and kitchen. We engaged a good team of builders, a project manager, a start date was agreed, and we were off! The first stage was to dig out the footings and new foundations for the extension but within the first hour of the work commencing the mini digger had cut through the main water pipe to our house and other properties on the estate. Everything stopped. The first error was a failure to identify the mains supplies as they crossed the plot of land.

Solomon, in Psalm 127, knew that building anything-family, community, fellowship, congregation, church-must have God's involvement, blessing and protection. He must be at the heart of anything that is undertaken. It is fruitless to undertaken anything without Him and can lead to frustration and needless toil. But if God is at the heart of the matter, then He will give His peace, rest, and sleep.

Unless the Lord builds a house, the work of the builders is wasted. Unless the Lord protects a city, guarding it with sentries will do no good.

It is useless for you to work so hard from early morning until late at night, anxiously working for food to eat; for God gives rest to his loved ones. Psalm 127 v 1-2 NLT

On the frieze at the north end of the great hall in our Leeds Town Hall are these same words, 'Except the Lord build the house they labour in vain that build it' and on the frieze at the south end of the hall are the words 'Except the Lord keep the city the watchman waketh but in vain'. The Victorian architects and designers may have wanted to put God in His central place in the city of Leeds.

The motto of the city of Edinburgh, Scotland, appearing on its crest, and the city's official documents, are the Latin words, Nisi Dominus Frusta, which again come from the first words of this psalm and mean 'Without the Lord, Frustration.' So perhaps if we wish to avoid frustration, exhaustion, efforts in our own strength, worry, fretting, endless planning, and similar unproductive stresses then let us build with our God as the only architect and designer.

PRAY
Build Your kingdom here, Let the darkness fear
Show Your mighty hand. Heal our streets and land
Set Your church on fire, Win this nation back
Change the atmosphere, Build Your kingdom here
We pray.

Come set Your rule and reign, In our hearts again
Increase in us we pray Unveil why we're made
Come set our hearts ablaze with hope
Like wildfire in our very souls Holy Spirit, come invade us now
We are Your Church And we need Your power
In us.

Our personal and ever watchful Father Psalm 139

O Lord, you have examined my heart and know everything about me. You know when I sit or stand. When far away you know my every thought. You chart the path ahead of me and tell me where to stop and rest. Every moment you know where I am. You know what I am going to say before I even say it. You both precede and follow me and place your hand of blessing on my head. This is too glorious, too wonderful to believe! I can never be lost to your Spirit! I can never get away from my God! You saw me before I was born and scheduled each day of my life before I began to breathe. Every day was recorded in your book! How precious it is, Lord, to realize that you are thinking about me constantly! Psalm 139 v 1-6, 16-18 TLB

After Psalm 23, this familiar Psalm of David, is perhaps one that is so beautifully memorable and close to our hearts. Our Father God is ever watchful, intimately involved with our lives, and deeply personal in the care and blessing that He has for each of us. He is fully acquainted with all I do, think, say, or feel. He knows all the days that have been appointed for me, and there is no shadow, darkness or 'lostness' that can hide me from His hand of blessing. My whole being was put together according to His wonderful, unique, colourful, design. 'When I was being formed in secret, and intricately and skilfully formed as if embroidered with many colours in the depths of the earth.' Verse 15

I can never be lost to His Spirit. I never need to hide from His presence. When the dark times come His loving presence surrounds and holds firm. Keep hold of these thoughts and never doubt the Father's love.

You are the peace of all things calm
You are the place to hide from harm
You are the light that shines in dark
You are the heart's eternal spark
You are the door that's open wide
You are the guest who waits inside
You are the stranger at the door
You are the calling of the poor
You are my Lord and with me still
You are my love, keep me from ill
You are the light, the truth, the way
You are my Saviour this very day.

(Celtic oral tradition - 1st millennium)

Restoration and Transformation Psalm 51

Create in me a clean heart, O God;
and renew a right spirit within me.
Cast me not away from thy presence;
and take not thy holy spirit from me.
Restore unto me the joy of thy salvation;
and uphold me with thy free spirit. Psalm 51 v 10-12 KJV

In this psalm, David acknowledges his sin before God-his sin in relation to Bathsheba, the murder of Uriah her husband, and his failures as leader and king. He is broken, he is honest, he has no excuses, no rationalisation of his actions, just a frank confession of sin. David pleads for God's forgiveness and restoration. David asks God to "cleanse me with hyssop, and I will be clean; wash me, and I will be whiter than snow. He needs a major heart and life transformation.

Being cleansed with hyssop is a significant phrase. Hyssop was often used as a symbol for cleansing and renewal and was used frequently in ceremonies and sacrifices. The blood of a lamb was painted on to door frames using hyssop by the Israelites, on the night they escaped from captivity in Egypt. Moses said, "Take a bunch of hyssop, dip it into the blood in the basin and put some of the blood on the top and on both sides of the doorframe." Exodus 12 v 22

At the crucifixion of Jesus, we read of the use of hyssop again. Jesus said, "I am thirsty." A jar of wine vinegar was there, so they soaked a sponge in it, put the sponge on a stalk of the hyssop plant, and lifted it to Jesus' lips. When he had received the drink, Jesus said, "It is finished." John 19 v 29-30

The death of Jesus and the shedding of His blood is the only way for us to have forgiveness, release, and restoration. As the perfect sacrifice, Hs blood was shed for us, so that we could be forgiven. He was the sacrificial lamb. Let us come to Jesus asking for His forgiveness. There is no other way.

I love the way that The Message version phrases a part of David's request. "God, make a fresh start in me, shape a Genesis week from the chaos of my life. Bring me back from grey exile, put a fresh wind in my sails!"

PRAY for a genesis week- a fresh beginning with His Spirit in our sails. - every new week

SONG
Sin separated
The breach was far too wide
But from the far side of the chasm
You held me in your sight.

So, you made a way
Across the great divide
Left behind Heaven's throne
To build it here inside.

And there at the cross
You paid the debt I owed
Broke my chains, freed my soul
For the first time I had hope.

Thank you, Jesus, for the blood applied
Thank you Jesus, it has washed me white
Thank you Jesus, you have saved my life
Brought me from the darkness into glorious light.

Charity Gayle

Psalm 61 v 1-2 A Psalm of David. KJV

Hear my cry, O God; attend unto my prayer. From the end of the earth will I cry unto thee, when my heart is overwhelmed: lead me to the rock that is higher than I.

As a young Christian, it was the King James Version of the Bible that I read, used, learned verses and parts by heart from, and managed to successfully remember. I love its poetry and style and found that it was somehow easier to remember it's phrases and verses. But I appreciate and love the more modern translations of God's word and find that they have new insights and lessons that pop out at me. So, as with Psalm 23 last week, here are some modern versions and transliterations of these most famous of words, that we may find helpful.

Lead me to the rock that is higher than I. A rock that is too high to reach without Your help. AMP

Carry me to a high rock where no one can reach me. You are my place of safety. ERV

O God, hear my prayer. Listen to my heart's cry. For no matter where I am, even when I'm far from home, I will cry out to you for a Father's help. When I'm feeble and overwhelmed by life, guide me to your glory, where I am safe and sheltered. Lord, you are a paradise of protection to me. You lift me high above the fray. None of my foes can touch me when I'm held firmly in your wraparound presence. TPT

When we have reached an end point, feeling overwhelmed, adrift, God not only listens to our prayer but 'attends' to it, acting, to lead us to that higher place of His presence and care.

LECTIO PRAYER

Father, help me to live this day to the full, being true to you in every way.

Jesus, help me to give myself away to others being kind to everyone I meet.

Spirit, help me to love the lost, proclaiming Christ in all I do and say. Amen.

Creation Songs David the Psalmist and Tagore (Gitanjali - Song offerings)

The whole earth is filled with awe at your wonders;
where morning dawns, where evening fades,
you call forth songs of joy. **Psalm 65 v 8 A song of David**

But let all who take refuge in you be glad;
let them ever sing for joy.
Spread your protection over them,
that those who love your name may rejoice in you. Psalm 5 v 11-12 David

David and other psalmists wrote the most amazing poetic works of praise to God. Psalm 104 is the most beautiful praise poem about the wonders of creation and our Creator God. *"The poem contains a complete cosmos: sea and land, cloud and sunlight, plant, and animal, light and darkness, life and death, are all proved to be expressive of the presence of the Lord." Charles Spurgeon.* Other poets and writers have been inspired to write poems, songs and prose about the wonders and joy of creation and the natural world around them. God's wonderful world speaks to many, and His creation calls forth songs of praise.

Rabindranath Tagore (1861-1941), a famous Indian writer, wrote a collection of songs, his Song Offerings or Gitanjali, which were published in 1912 in his native language of Bengali. He was awarded the Nobel Prize for Literature in 1913 for these songs. Many of Tagore's poems point to creation and the sights and sounds that transported him to a higher plain and his songs were also set to music as were David's. I must apologise here for quoting from a Hindu writer, but Tagore's songs are very reminiscent of David's Psalms of praise and worship. Both writers share a leaning towards a higher power who transforms a failing heart into a worshipping heart, that forgets himself and can call his lord his friend.

"When thou commandest me to sing it seems that

My heart would break with pride; and I look to Thy face,

And tears come to my eyes.

All that is harsh and dissonant in my life melts

into one sweet harmony-and my adoration

spreads wings like a glad bird on its flight across the sea.

I know that thou takest pleasure in my singing.

I know that only as a singer I come before thy presence.

I touch by the edge of the far spreading wing of my song

thy feet which I never could aspire to reach.

Drunk with the joy of singing I forget myself

and call thee friend who art my lord."

A Song Tagore

The God that we know through Jesus is to be honoured above all. The man-made gods of the nations are false and empty. Psalm 96 says:

Sing to the Lord a new song. Let all the earth sing to the Lord. Sing to the Lord. Honour His name. Make His saving power known from day to day. Tell of His shining-greatness among the nations. Tell of His wonderful works among all the people. For the Lord is great and should be given much praise. He is to be honoured with fear above all gods. For all the gods of the nations are false gods. But the Lord made the heavens. Honour and great power are with Him. Strength and beauty are in His holy place. Psalm 96 v 1-6

May we always sing for joy because this Creator God is the God whom we love and serve.

Mother Theresa

Nothingness and fullness

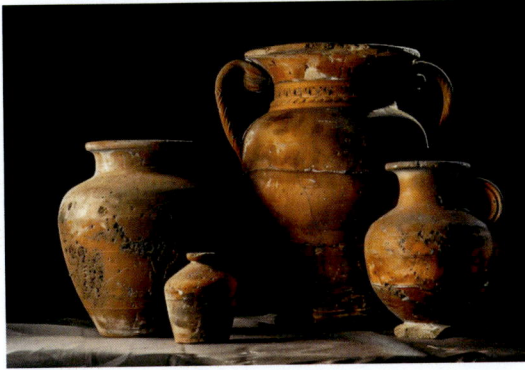

"When we have nothing to give, let us give Him that nothingness. Let us all remain as empty as possible so that God can fill us. Even God cannot fill what is already full. God won't force Himself on us. You are filling the world with the love God has given you." Mother Teresa

I often feel as if 'I am running on empty,' or on 'the bottom of the tank.' It is not a comfortable place to be. I feel to be lacking in energy with nothing to give to others. My supply has dried up. So, the account of the widow and her 'nothingness' is an encouragement.

The widow in 2 Kings 4 was in a desperate situation and about to lose her two sons into the slavery of her late husband's creditors. The widow appealed for help to Elisha as she said, "I have nothing", but a small jar, a drop of oil. Elisha instructed her to borrow as many empty jars, bowls, jugs, and containers as possible, from her friends and neighbours. Elisha said, "Go around and ask all your neighbours for empty jars. Don't ask for just a few." When she had collected all these containers together, she began to pour her tiny amount of oil into each of them in turn. Her sons kept bringing the jars to her, and she filled one after another as the oil kept pouring and multiplying. Soon every container was full to the brim! The widow went from having nothing and being empty, to being full, full to the brim, with the oil by which she would be able to create an income for herself and her sons.

The widow did not have 'nothing.' She had something. She had a tiny jug of oil, friends and neighbours, and her connection to Elisha.

Out of his fullness we have all received grace in place of grace already given. John 1 v 16

I pray that out of his glorious riches he may strengthen you with power through his Spirit in your inner being, so that Christ may dwell in your hearts through faith. And I pray that you, being rooted and established in love, may have power, together with all the Lord's holy people, to grasp how wide and long and high and deep is the love of Christ, and to know this love that surpasses knowledge – that you may be filled to the measure of all the fullness of God. Paul's prayer Ephesians 3 v 16-19 NIV

"If you are discouraged, it is a sign of pride because it shows you trust in your own power. Your self-sufficiency, your selfishness, and your intellectual pride will inhibit His coming to live in your heart because God cannot fill what is already full. It is as simple as that." Mother Teresa

PRAY
Father, when I feel that I have nothing, that I am empty, please remind me that you have the resources and the strength, not me. Please fill me with your love.

Ordinary and Extraordinary

"Do not imagine that love, to be true, must be extraordinary. No, what we need in our love is the continuity to love the One we love. See how a lamp burns, by the continual consumption of little drops of oil. If there are no more of these drops in the lamp, there will be no light."

"What are these drops of oil in our lamps? They are the little things of everyday life- fidelity, little words of kindness, just a little thought for others, those little acts of silence, of look, and thought, of word and deed." Mother Teresa

Our society, community, church, and homes, need little drops of kindness, compassion, gentleness, understanding, and love- lots of little drops of love. Love can be 'small.' It doesn't have to be 'big,' grand, and showy. We need the kind of love that Paul spoke of in 1 Corinthians 13. It can sometimes be easy to do that small act of kindness, to be generous with a thoughtful gift, encourage with a gentle word, or be patient with a troublesome family member, neighbour, or friend. But as I read again the quotation from Mother Teresa, I realize that these qualities of kindness, love, gentleness, and selflessness need to come from a very deep, inner place. These drops of love are most effective when they come from a place of knowing and loving a gentle Saviour who has begun to change our inner being. There is a continuity to loving others which comes from loving Him first. This oil should flow from a love that we experience and receive from Jesus. This kind of love is hard to manufacture and sustain in any other way. This kind of love is an extraordinary love.

Love never gives up.
Love cares more for others than for self.
Love doesn't want what it doesn't have.
Love doesn't strut, Doesn't have a swelled head,
Doesn't force itself on others, Isn't always "me first,"
Doesn't fly off the handle, Doesn't keep score of the sins of others,
Doesn't revel when others grovel,
Takes pleasure in the flowering of truth,
Puts up with anything,
Trusts God always,
Always looks for the best,
Never looks back,
But keeps going to the end. Love never dies.

I Corinthians 13 MSG

Be gentle with one another, sensitive. Forgive one another as quickly and thoroughly as God in Christ forgave you. Ephesians 4 v 32 MSG

PRAY

My oil is running low and so the light is flickering. Remind me that your love is new every morning and that your compassions fail not. Touch me again in that deep, inner place.

An Understanding Love

The greatest poverty in the world is not the want of food but the want of love. Mother Teresa

Open your eyes and see. There is not just hunger for a piece of bread. There is hunger for understanding love, for the word of God. Nakedness is not only for a piece of cloth. Nakedness is the loss of human dignity. The loss of that beautiful virtue of purity which is so misused nowadays. Mother Teresa

I love this phrase an" understanding love." As part of training sessions on crossing cultures before working abroad, you are trained to be sensitive to differences when speaking, working, and living with those of other languages and cultures. You put on 'cultural glasses', see, and experience the world as the other person sees and experiences it, and step into their shoes. You learn to be perceptive, intuitive, with sensitivity to the other person's life experience. This kind of empathy and discernment creates connections. Whenever we meet and speak with another person, we need that sensitivity to really 'see' the other person with the unspoken languages of mood, movement, expressions, and the many other clues that we can interpret.

I love to read the accounts of Jesus meeting with individuals in the Gospels where He demonstrates most powerfully this 'understanding love.' When Jesus meets the Samaritan woman at the well, He creates an opening, a safe place for her, recognizing her deep needs. His approach is tender, kind, His questioning sensitive, and insightful as He listens to her responses. He sees that she is searching for a deeper understanding and begins to help her focus. Catching the depth of her situation and longing for change, He creates the potential for a new perspective and then leads her forward. His understanding and perception of her, is deep and focussed. Jesus is the model of empathy, insight, and compassion.

We all value and need this kind of 'understanding love'. We all seek to be listened to, loved, and understood. Lots of words are not needed. Being listened to, given time, and being understood, are powerful healers.

Love in Action. *Love must be sincere. Hate what is evil; cling to what is good. Be devoted to one another in love. Honour one another above yourselves. Never be lacking in zeal, but keep your spiritual fervour, serving the Lord. Be joyful in hope, patient in affliction, faithful in prayer. Share with the Lord's people who are in need. Practice hospitality. Bless those who persecute you; bless and do not curse. Rejoice with those who rejoice; mourn with those who mourn. Live in harmony with one another. Do not be proud, but be willing to associate with people of low position. Do not be conceited. Romans 12 v 8-16 NIV*

But the Lord said to Samuel, The Lord does not look at the things people look at. People look at the outward appearance, but the Lord looks at the heart. 1 Samuel 16 v 7 NIV

PRAY
Father, help us to be available to others. Help us to look beyond the person's words, situation and appearance, and to see to their heart and need- with an understanding love.

Channels, instruments, or both?

In Luke 4, at the start of Jesus's ministry and mission, Jesus announced His call to serve. His mission was to the poor, the rejected, the marginalised, those without power or position, and this calling would take Him to the cross.

The Spirit of the Lord is upon me,
*   for he has anointed me to bring Good News to the poor.*
He has sent me to proclaim that captives will be released,
*   that the blind will see,*
that the oppressed will be set free,
*   and that the time of the Lord's favour has come. Luke 4 v 18 NLT*

Mother Teresa had been called to follow Christ, age 18, but she believed that she had been given a special call, aged 37, 'a call within a call' to serve the poor and the rejected, and she spent her years in Kolkata, India and beyond, fulfilling this call. She is not universally admired and in fact had many critics, but she was perhaps both an instrument for God, and a channel of His love and grace.

"I do not think I have any special qualities. I don't claim anything for the work. It is his work. I am like a little pencil in His hand, that is all. He does the thinking. He does the writing. The pencil has nothing to do with it. The pencil has only to be allowed to be used". Mother Teresa

"We are not channels; we are instruments. Channels give nothing of their own they just let water run through them. In our action, we are instruments in God's hand, and he writes beautifully." Mother Teresa

I have struggled this week with these two terms- a channel and an instrument- that God chooses to use. The song 'make me a channel of your peace' instantly comes to mind. Perhaps another key word is 'available.' God has given each of us unique temperaments, gifts, abilities, circumstances, and He desires His love and message to flow through us. There may be times when we are 'active', have a specific role, job description, and we may know that we are in 'active service' for Him. At other times we may feel that we can only just 'be'. But at all times we reflect His love and grace and are his channels. Channels do give much of themselves-they are not blank and empty. May we be available to our risen Christ and willing for Him to use us in any way that He chooses. Whatever He does, He does it beautifully.

The king's heart is like channels of water in the hand of the Lord; He turns it whichever way He wishes. Proverbs 21 v 1 AMP

For we are His workmanship [His own master work, a work of art], created in Christ Jesus [reborn from above—spiritually transformed, renewed, ready to be used] for good works, which God prepared [for us] beforehand [taking paths which He set], so that we would walk in them [living the good life which He prearranged and made ready for us]. Ephesians 2 v 10 AMP

A broken pencil

As a teacher of very small children, one of my least desirable tasks, an almost daily task, was the sharpening of the pencils. Often, this task was completed in the ancient, slow way with the old-fashioned pencil sharpener, which tended to hurt the fingers. This was until I was able to invest in an electric pencil sharpener, which proved to be a far superior and faster method of sharpening. We had a delivery of new pencils only at the beginning of each term and so towards the end of the term, the pencils were chewed, small, often ineffective, and could no longer be sharpened. Also, towards the end of the term, we suffered from 'the disappearance of the red pencils.' The red pencils were the most popular and always the first to be sharpened down to nothingness, and this was a major problem as we approached Christmas, as then the red pencil was in great demand. For the Standard Assessment Tests in class, we had the luxury of being given a class set of brand-new pencils- pristine, sharp, and perfect. No sharpening needed. As an old-fashioned style of teacher, I preferred the children in my care to write with properly sharpened pencils or how else could they write their perfect cursive script, achieve their Pen Handwriting Certificate, and progress on to using the Berol Handwriting Pen?

Mother Teresa writes "I always say I am a little pencil in God's hands. He does the thinking. He does the writing. He does everything and sometimes it is hard because it is a broken pencil, and He has to sharpen it a little more. Be a little instrument in His hands so that He can use you anytime, anywhere. We have only to say, 'yes' to God".

Mother Teresa perhaps refers here to her personal need of having the rough edges smoothed away and being sharpened ready for the service of God. Mother Teresa had dark periods in her Christian living, doubts, and fears. Some of these times were disclosed in her private diaries released after her death. She may have had her personal struggles as we all do and yet she knew that God was still able to use her in mighty ways- even as a broken pencil.

For each of us, God is changing us all the time, smoothing off the rough edges so that we may become even more useful to Him. This is a continual process and can be uncomfortable and sometimes painful. But He is changing us gradually so that we become more like Jesus. God has also placed us in His church as we need others to help us with this process. I once heard the phrase 'sandpaper people' referring to those people who may have the habit of 'rubbing us up the wrong way'. These folk, and our closest Christian friends and colleagues who know us well, are perfectly placed to help us sharpen off the rough edges.

But we all, with open face beholding as in a glass the glory of the Lord, are changed into the same image from glory to glory, even as by the Spirit of the Lord. 2 Corinthians 3 v 18 KJV

As iron sharpens iron,
so one person sharpens another. Proverbs 27 v 17 NIRV

PRAY
Father God, I often feel ineffective, and not as 'useable' as the next person. Sometimes, I feel worn down and not ready or willing to be used. I need your encouragement, and help. In your hand, I can do whatever you purpose for me. Thank you.

Prayer

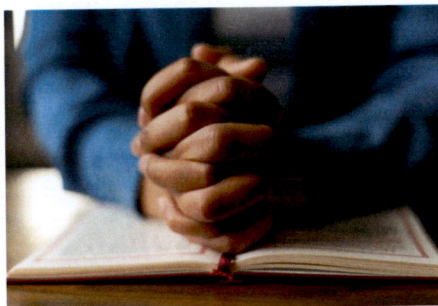

This week, I have been aware of my need for the prayer support of my Christian family and friends. There are times when we hit a situation or concern and we do not have the personal resources or energy to be able to deal with it adequately, and so at such times we reach out to our praying friends to support us through such a tough time. They can pray for us when we cannot. At other times, we may be the ones to support others in this way. Sometimes just an 'arrow prayer' or the very simplest and shortest of prayers only is required. Long wordy prayers are not needed. Thankfully God can read our hearts and knows the situation that we are struggling with. So, I am thankful for this reminder from Mother

Teresa about prayer. I am so thankful that she commended short prayers from the heart.

"Perfect prayer does not consist of many words but in the fervour of the desire which raises the heart to Jesus.

You can pray while you work. Work doesn't stop prayer and prayer doesn't stop work. It requires only that small raising of the mind to Him. I love you God. I trust you. I believe in you. I need you now. Small things like that. They are wonderful prayers". Mother Teresa

Don't fret or worry. Instead of worrying, pray. Let petitions and praises shape your worries into prayers, letting God know your concerns. Before you know it, a sense of God's wholeness, everything coming together for good, will come and settle you down. It's wonderful what happens when Christ displaces worry at the centre of your life. Philippians 4 v 6 MSG

Phil and I have had the privilege of having Christian supporters and 'prayers' over the many years that we have walked with Jesus. There have been, and there still are today, those faithful people 'who have our back,' who know us, and our changing situations very well. We became Christians as teenagers and we have the privilege of still being in contact with the man who was our Youth Leader many, many years ago. He guided, trained, and supported us in those early days of our Christian walk, and remains our trusted confidante and prayer supporter. He faithfully prays for us and has supported us through some challenging times. We are so thankful to have someone who is a person of prayer, still involved in our lives. *The earnest prayer of a righteous man has great power and wonderful results. James 5 v 16 TLB*

We should never underestimate the effectiveness of our prayers and those of others. Prayers are like incense offered up to the Father. David prayed- "May my prayer be set before you like incense; may the lifting up of my hands be like the evening sacrifice". *Psalm 141 v 2*

"The smoke of the incense, together with the prayers of God's people, went up before God from the angel's hand". *Revelation 8 v 4 NIV*

PRAY
Help us to be sensitive to the needs of others.

Teach us how to pray for others and not to focus on ourselves.

Help us to be gentle, approachable, and kind so that others may be comfortable in asking for support and prayer. Amen

What a Friend we have in Jesus,
All our sins and griefs to bear!
What a privilege to carry,
Everything to God in prayer!
Oh, what peace we often forfeit,
Oh, what needless pain we bear.
All because we do not carry
Everything to God in prayer!
Joseph Medlicott Scriven

Home and Homelessness

Home is a wonderful word. Home is not four walls and a roof, or just a residence or structure made of different materials. Home is so much more. Home is our haven, our place of shelter, rest and refuge, our place of peace, where we learn what is important, what matters, and where memories are made. A place to call home is a fundamental need, where we feel safe and secure. "The ache for home lives in all of us, the safe place where we can go as we are and not be questioned."

It is so sad that so many people do not possess such a safe haven of their own. In every culture, country and society, there are those who are homeless or moving from one temporary dwelling to another. As we watch our news screens now, we see images of families escaping from fighting, civil war, bombing and horrors in Khartoum, Sudan. They are leaving their home, abandoning all that they know, to find a place of safety in a neighbouring country.

Mother Teresa spoke directly and poignantly about homelessness and the refugee crisis. "The tide of human suffering grows even greater. This is especially so of those who are refugees. This is a special kind of suffering. Not only are they forced to suffer famine, persecution, war, and natural disaster, but also the horrific plight of being forced to keep on the move. They have nowhere which they can call home and often no one is prepared to listen to their cry for help".

During the three years of Jesus's ministry, Jesus spent time in people's homes-many people's homes. I am sure that Jesus knew the value of home. He was a regular visitor to the homes of Simon Peter, Lazarus, Matthew Levi, and Zacchaeus, but He also enjoyed hospitality in the home of Simon the Pharisee, and other prominent Pharisees. Jesus's reputation was that He spent time with tax collectors and sinners in their homes. Jesus also knew those who had no home. The demon possessed man in the land of the Gerasene's had no clothes to wear and he had no home. The tombs were his only home. Yet, after Jesus heals him, and he is restored, Jesus says, "Return home and tell how much God has done for you." He was told to go home, perhaps to his family, and his community, and gave testimony to the power of Jesus.

"There is plenty of room for you in my Father's home. If that weren't so, would I have told you that I'm on my way to get a room ready for you? And if I'm on my way to get your room ready, I'll come back and get you so you can live where I live." John 14 v 2-3 MSG

Jesus replied, "All who love me will do what I say. My Father will love them, and we will come and make our home with each of them. John 14 v 23 NIV

For this world is not our home; we are looking forward to our everlasting home in heaven. Hebrews 13 v 14 TLB

PRAY

Father, help us to have a truer perspective of 'home.' May we look forward to our home of the future while we are at 'home' here. We pray for those in Sudan who are desperately running away from their home to find safe shelter, in a neighbouring country, and away from civil war and threat to life. Be with those who are on the move.

"Home is where one starts from." –T.S. Eliot

God- flavours and God-colours

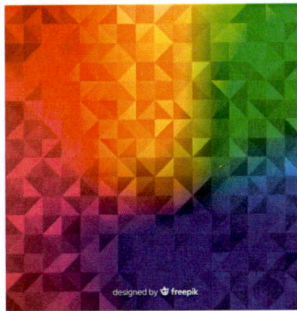

designed by freepik

Our church had three key statements that signified the values and beliefs of our fellowship. The key principles or values were to love God, to follow Jesus and to live generously. In His sermon on the mount, Jesus gave very clear instructions about how we should live in relationship with other people. Jesus' desire for us was that we should bring out the God colours in the world, live openly and generously with our lives, share who we are and what we have, and be fully open to others. We were to live out our God given identity and live generously and graciously towards every person in our sphere of life and influence, regardless of their status or position.

In a word, what I'm saying is, Grow up. You're kingdom subjects. Now live like it. Live out your God-created identity. Live generously and graciously toward others, the way God lives toward you. Matthew 5 v 46 MSG

So, I have been considering how this living generously might look and once again, some familiar words from Mother Teresa seemed relevant here.

"The greatest poverty in the world is not the want of food but the want of love. The poverty of the heart is often more difficult to relieve and to defeat."

When we look carefully enough, we can see the great needs, sorrows, loneliness, burdens and struggles of people around us. We can see people who are struggling with poverty of heart, mind and spirit, and the ache of loneliness. When people are feeling grey, drab, empty, weary, stale, and flat, we are to step alongside and bring the God colours to them. When people are feeling hollow, in need, with aching, empty hearts and spirits, we are to help them to taste the God flavours. We are to come near, to 'open up' and to share the love that we have received in Christ. Then perhaps they will 'open up' to the love of our generous multicoloured, multifaceted God.

Let me tell you why you are here. You're here to be salt-seasoning that brings out the God-flavours of this earth. If you lose your saltiness, how will people taste godliness? You've lost your usefulness and will end up in the garbage. Here's another way to put it: You're here to be light, bringing out the God-colours in the world. God is not a secret to be kept. We're going public with this, as public as a city on a hill. If I make you light bearers, you don't think I'm going to hide you under a bucket, do you? I'm putting you on a light stand. Now that I've put you there on a hilltop, on a light stand—shine! Keep open house; be generous with your lives. By opening up to others, you'll prompt people to open up with God, this generous Father in heaven. Matthew 5 v 13-16 MSG

PRAY

Father God, people are hungry for love, for acceptance, for a place to belong. For those who are empty, please fill them. For those who are lonely, please send someone, a family, a safe place. Help us to see those people who are experiencing a 'poverty of the heart' by the help of your Spirit. May we be the answer to our own prayer and live generously. Give us a heart to serve. Amen

One person at a time

"We ourselves feel that what we are doing, is just a drop in the ocean. But if that drop was not there, I think the ocean would be less by that missing drop. We don't have to think in numbers. We can only love one person at a time, serve one person at a time."   Mother Teresa

Jesus

Our 'Personal' Saviour

"I am gentle and humble in heart."

Our Saviour is someone who comes close to the individual. He walks alongside and talks, He sits with someone and listens, He fully understands the situation and their feelings, He sits at the meal table and shares in the conversation, and He demonstrates "the unforced rhythms of grace." He says, "Keep company with me and you'll learn to live freely and lightly." I love these words of the Father that Jesus Himself used to describe His ministry, words from Isaiah 42 v 1-4.

Look well at my handpicked servant;
  I love him so much, take such delight in Him.
I've placed my Spirit on him;
  He'll decree justice to the nations.
But He won't yell, won't raise his voice;
  there'll be no commotion in the streets.
He won't walk over anyone's feelings,
  won't push you into a corner.
Before you know it, His justice will triumph;
  the mere sound of His name will signal hope, even
 among far-off unbelievers. MSG

Jesus sat at the well in Samaria taking a lower place as He talked with the woman. This would have been an unheard-of thing to do. The unfamiliar Jew would have stood a distance away with an air of authority and perhaps disdain. But no, Jesus took the low place to engage and not to alarm. He knew her needs, thoughts, aspirations, and the extent of her searching. When a woman was healed secretly, touching the hem of Jesus's garment, Jesus called her to come to Him, not to embarrass her publicly, but to call her 'daughter.' He said to her, 'Daughter, your faith has healed you. Go in peace and be freed from your suffering.' "At Bethsaida, some people brought a blind man and begged Jesus to touch Him. He took the blind man by the hand and led him outside the village. When he had spat on the man's eyes and put his hands on him, Jesus asked, 'Do you see anything? Jesus took the man to a quiet place, outside of the village, away from prying eyes, and used a clay mixture on his eyes as a unique method of healing. Perhaps He knew that this individual needed that human touch, that tangible, physical method of healing. An individual response to a needy individual.

Jesus walked alongside the two disciples on the road to Emmaus engaging in their conversation. He opened the conversation, judging their current understanding of the events in Jerusalem, giving them space and time to clarify their thoughts, to talk and to share. After the resurrection, Jesus seemed to return intentionally for Thomas, who had been absent when Jesus had first appeared at the upper room. Jesus understood perfectly where Thomas was coming from and spoke graciously and gently.

There are so many examples of Jesus dealing gently with individuals, fully understanding them with His perfect empathy and knowledge. This is our Saviour. The gentle, personal Saviour.

Jesus distributes the bread

Our Jewish friends and neighbours are getting ready to celebrate Pesach or Passover which is one of their most important festivals remembering their release from slavery in Egypt into freedom. Jesus and His disciples had prepared their Passover meal, and it was on this night that Judas would leave the meal table and inform the authorities about Jesus's plans and location in readiness for them to arrest Him. It is strikingly significant, that Jesus, knowing that Judas would betray Him, shared the meal with Judas as one of His twelve, distributing the bread and the wine to him. "But the hand of him who is going to betray me is with mine on the table". **Luke 22 v 21** At the Passover meal when the unleavened bread is lifted to be broken the following traditional words would be spoken "This is the bread of affliction which our fathers ate in the land of Egypt. Let everyone who hungers come and eat; let everyone who is needy come and eat the Passover meal." Jesus's love was reaching out to Judas.

After the resurrection of Jesus, two disciples walking to Emmaus, were joined by Him on the road. Jesus spoke to them of many things, but they failed to recognise Him. It was only when they invited Him to share their meal and the way that He broke the bread and gave thanks, that their eyes were opened. 'So, he went home with them. As they sat down to eat, he took the bread and blessed it. Then he broke it and gave it to them. Suddenly, their eyes were opened, and they recognized him.' **Luke 24 v 29-31 NLT** It was the breaking of the bread that was significant. There was a sudden moment of clarity! The stranger is Jesus.

At the last supper, Jesus introduced a new covenant. This meal was to be shared by all who chose to follow Jesus. This meal would signify freedom from the old, from sin and the judgement of the law to a new relationship of freedom, forgiveness, and grace. The price would be paid; sins dealt with, and a new meal prepared for all who are hungry and needy. 'While they were eating, Jesus took bread, and when he had given thanks, he broke it and gave it to his disciples, saying, "Take and eat; this is my body. "Then he took a cup, and when he had given thanks, he gave it to them, saying, "Drink from it, all of you. This is my blood of the covenant, which is poured out for many for the forgiveness of sins. **Matthew 26 v 26-28**

When Jesus fed the five thousand and the four thousand with bread in a miraculous way, He distributed the bread to the disciples, and they distributed the bread to the gathered crowds. I often wonder at what point did the miracle occur. Where did the multiplication happen? I tend to think that it was as soon as the bread and the fish left the hands of Jesus. But He gave the bread to the disciples, and they shared out, apportioned the food, handed it out to others. They had their part to play. This perhaps is a lovely picture of our communion service when the bread and the wine is served out to the congregation.

Jesus longs to feed the hungry and the needy. "I am the bread of life," Jesus told them. "Those who come to me will never be hungry; those who believe in me will never be thirsty. **John 6 v 35 GNT** Jesus has paid the full price but perhaps we may help to take the bread to the hungry and those who are in need.

Break Thou the Bread of Life,
  Dear Lord, to me,
As Thou didst break the loaves
  Beside the sea;
Beyond the sacred page
  I seek Thee, Lord;
My spirit pants for Thee,
  O Living Word.

Lyrics by Mary Artemesia Lathbury (1841-1913)

Planting Peace

I am very poor at growing anything green. It might be seeds, houseplants, plants for the garden or vegetables. I can succeed with cress and hardy perennials such as lavender, but little else. My father was a member of a horticultural society, and we had a garden and a large allotment which we looked after every weekend, but I am afraid that I did not absorb his many gardening skills. But I am encouraged to be a planter of peace. Our world is a very troubled place and, in 2024 on our screens we have witnessed wars, disasters, heartaches, mental health crises in our young people and much more. So, as we enter a new year, may we endeavour to be planters of peace, whether we feel capable, skilled or woefully inadequate. May we offer love, joy, gentleness, along with peace, as we connect with others in our everyday. Help us to share the peace of the Prince of Peace.

A Prayer for Planting Peace

(In the style of the prayer of St Francis of Assisi)

By Lizzie Ojo Martens

Lord as I reflect on the challenges present within my community

As well as my own lived experience,

I ask that you make me an instrument of your peace.

Where there is division, let me sow unity.

Where there is stigma, belonging.

Where there is unfamiliarity, awareness.

Where there is sorrow, joy.

Where there is silence or shame, light.

Where there is isolation, inclusion and companionship.

Where there is hopelessness, hope.

O Divine Counsellor, grant that I may not so much seek to be comforted, but to comfort others

And to speak, as to listen.

For it is in giving that we receive,

And it is in your presence that we find peace.

For a child is born to us,
  a son is given to us.
The government will rest on his shoulders.
  And he will be called:
Wonderful Counsellor, Mighty God,
  Everlasting Father, Prince of Peace.
His government and its peace
  will never end. Isaiah 9 v 6-7 NLT

In John 14 v 27 Jesus offers His shalom' peace. He 'bequeaths'' His peace. Just as a rich person would bequeath property or something valuable to someone else, the peace of Jesus is bequeathed to us Jesus offers wholeness, completeness, soundness of spirit, soul and body, and wellbeing. This is His gift to us. Let us share this gift.

SONG
Let there be peace on earth
And let it begin with me
Let there be peace on Earth
The peace that was meant to be

Let peace begin with me
Let this be the moment now.

With every step I take
Let this be my solemn vow
To take each moment and live
Each moment in peace eternally
Let there be peace on earth
And let it begin with me

Songwriters: Jill Jackson & Sy Miller

Let There Be Peace on Earth lyrics © Music Copyright Consultant Grp

Everything

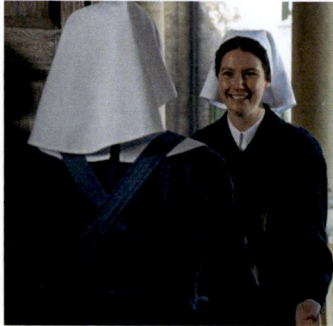

© BBC

I am a great fan of the BBC Series Call the Midwife, and in its most recent episode, we see a new, trainee midwife, Sister Catherine, join Nonnatus House. Sister Catherine, also a nun, is to complete her training as a midwife. Sister Monica Joan, an older, experienced nurse and Nun seeks out Sister Catherine, bringing her a plateful of chocolate digestive biscuits. I wonder if this is a test given by the 'ancient' Nun knowing that they should not eat between meals. However, a deep, and searching conversation follows. She is asked if this is the life that she imagined, and she reflects it is the life she has been called to. She didn't imagine much. She just listened to God's voice – and God is a persuasive speaker. When asked what God asked her to surrender, she replies "Everything". But the older sister counsels that everything is simply a word, it is like a single suitcase into which we bundle all we are.

Sister Catherine then reflects what her own 'everything' consists of -"my time, pear drops, my cat Maude, mascara, trampolining, coffee in the percolator, my brothers and sisters, waking up in my flat with my friends. Choosing what to wear, choosing what to eat, choosing what to do. Sometimes, I miss choosing most of all." Sister Monica then tells her, that's your everything now – but that there is so much more.

I thought about that word 'everything.' It is rare for someone to relinquish, surrender their rights or to give up their control of something. It would usually apply to property rights, part of an inheritance, or in rare occasions, the rights to the care of a child. Sister Monica Joan was born into a wealthy, aristocratic family who had disapproved of her choice of a Midwifery career and even more so of her being a Nun, taking her vow of poverty. Sister Catherine, at the beginning of her own journey, was honest about the challenge of 'letting go,' and the right to choose for herself.

We sometimes sing the old hymn 'I surrender all.' I find it immensely difficult to sing this hymn. It is hard to relinquish control, to ignore our material 'stuff,' and things that we like to have around us. We have our home, our car, our salary, our pensions, our holidays, the electronic devises that connect us to family and others. We have daily plans, schedules, and the things which entertain.

All to Jesus I surrender
All to Him I freely give
I will ever love and trust Him
In His presence daily live

All to Jesus I surrender
Humbly at His feet I bow
Worldly pleasures all forsaken
Take me, Jesus, take me now.

Immediately after Jesus was baptized, He was taken into the desert for a time of severe testing. In the third and final test Jesus was taken to a very high mountain, shown all the kingdoms of the world, their magnificence, and their delights, the devil, announcing, "everything there I will give you, if you will fall down and worship me." "Away with you, Satan!" replied Jesus, "the scripture says, 'You shall worship the Lord your God, and Him only you shall serve'." Matthew 4 v 8-11 NIV

The devil offered Jesus 'everything.' Everything can be yours, but only if you will worship me.

Jesus was tested to the extreme, which gives me hope that He understands my struggles, my confused priorities, my muddled thinking, my pressures and my weakness

PRAY
What do I hang on to at all costs? What time swallowing task could I let go of?

Jesus, shape my life so that it may more resemble yours. Prune my priorities and desires.

Safe and Sound

The idiom 'safe and sound' is a wonderful phrase that conjures up other words such as secure, home, free from anxiety, safety, settled and established. I love going away on holiday, but I am a 'home bird' now and at the end of a break I am ready to come home. When our own teenager with the group of Scouts returned from ten days of camping, trekking, and glacier walking in the Alps, we were thankful to have him home 'safe and sound' at the end of the expedition.

In the very familiar story of the prodigal son, we read that when the younger son was alone, without means of support, hungry, with no one to give him either help or food, he came to his senses and then he came home to his father. The phrase 'safe and sound' stands out in the story. One of the servants explains to the elder brother, the reason for the music, dancing and celebration. "Your brother has come,' he replied, 'and your father has killed the fattened calf because he has him back safe and sound." Luke 15 v 27 The father also explains his reasons for the feasting, the best cloak, the ring and the shoes gifted to his son. "We had to celebrate this happy day. For your brother was dead and has come back to life! He was lost, but now he is found!' Luke 15 v 33

We do not know how long the prodigal had been away from the family home, but the impression would be for an extremely long time-certainly months or even years. Without news of the son, the father in his worst moments, may have assumed that his son could have died in some far country. But he was now 'safe and sound', secure in the family and the home.

I often think of the story title more as 'the waiting, loving father.' The father who is constantly on the lookout for a returning son, his eyes monitoring that road home. The father who never gave up hope and who longed to wrap his arms around his youngest child. The father who ran towards his returning son to welcome him back-home before anyone else, such as the town elders could turn him away.

Our Heavenly Father is constantly on the lookout for us to come home to Him, -to be safe, sound, and secure in Him. He welcomes us back no matter what kind of condition we are in. He wants us to be free from all fear, and anxiety, and simply to come near to His heart of compassion.

As Moses, the 'man of God', was about to die, he gave each of the tribes of Israel a special blessing. His blessing to the tribe of Bejamin is particularly poignant. Let us claim this blessing for ourselves. Know that you are beloved of God, surrounded with His loving care and preserved from harm. You are safe in the father's embrace.

Concerning the tribe of Benjamin, Moses said: "He is beloved of God and lives in safety beside him. God surrounds him with his loving care, and preserves him from every harm." Deuteronomy 33 v 12 TLB

He is risen!

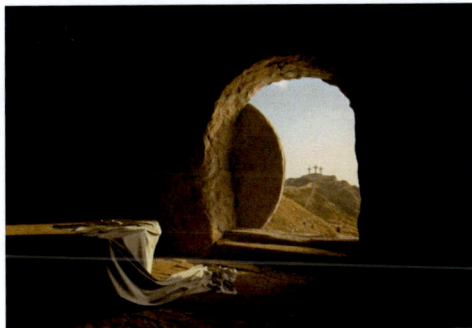

With great power the apostles gave witness to the resurrection of the Lord Jesus, and God poured rich blessings on them all. Acts 4 v 33 GNT

I pray that you will know how great His power is for those who have put their trust in Him. It is the same power that raised Christ from the dead. This same power put Christ at God's right side in heaven. Ephesians 1 v 19-20 NIV

As a young Christian, the book, Who Moved the Stone? By Frank Morison. (Faber and Faber, 1930) had a significant impact on me. In this book, Morison, a sceptic concerning Jesus and His resurrection, delivers a careful, historical study of the sequence of events between Jesus' entry into Jerusalem, the accounts of 'Holy Week 'and the resurrection, and the characters involved, which caused him to come to a very different place and to write a very different book to the one he originally intended. It was impossible for him to deny that the stone had been rolled away, that the tomb was empty and that the disciples, those first Christians and then thousands of new believers, were transformed and empowered because of their sure conviction of the resurrection of Jesus. It was this dramatic transformation of the early followers that perhaps had the greatest impact on him. The disciples had met with Jesus on several occasions after his resurrection. It was the presence of Jesus with them which powered them to spread the news far and wide, despite all opposition.

May we experience this same powerful transformation-the same power that raised Jesus from the tomb.

PRAY

Loving Jesus, as we celebrate Easter, renew our faith, and refresh our spirits. May the impact of your resurrection inspire us to live with conviction, share your love with others, and walk in the light of your truth. May we be faithful, reflecting your glory in all we do. Help us carry your message of love, hope, and redemption into the world. Amen.

SONG

What gift of grace is Jesus my redeemer
There is no more for heaven now to give
He is my joy, my righteousness, and freedom
My steadfast love, my deep and boundless peace.

To this I hold, my hope is only Jesus
For my life is wholly bound to His

Oh how strange and divine, I can sing, "All is mine"
Yet not I, but through Christ in me.

No fate I dread, I know I am forgiven
The future sure, the price it has been paid
For Jesus bled and suffered for my pardon
And He was raised to overthrow the grave.

Yet Not I but Through Christ in Me lyrics © Farren Love and War Publishing, Integrity's Alleluia! Music, Cityalight Music

Easter Reflection

As I have been reading the Easter accounts again, I have tried to place myself into the shoes of some of the key players and to imagine what impact the events of that brutal Roman crucifixion and the resurrection of Jesus would have on their lives. What would they do next? Would the resurrection transform their lives? Would they be changed?

Some of the transformations we know about. Judas Iscariot with his shame, horror, and dreadful betrayal and death. Mary Magdalene, John and Peter who were first at the empty tomb. But what of the Roman soldiers gambling for the clothes and tunic of a 'Jewish criminal? Simon of Cyrene, of North Africa, a strong man, coming home from work, forced to carry the cross for Jesus. A Roman Centurion, at the foot of the cross and standing guard over the brutal proceedings, making his first faith declaration, *"This has to be the Son of God!"* Two high ranking Jewish officials working together to prepare the body of Jesus for burial. Joseph of Arimathea, a member of the Sanhedrin, had risked his position and reputation to publicly identify with a criminal and to request of the Roman Governor, Pilate, that he should take the body of Jesus from the cross and place it for burial in his tomb, having already purchased a linen shroud. Nicodemus, a wealthy, influential Jew, brought the expensive burial spices, myrrh and aloes, with which to anoint the body of Jesus. Working together, Joseph and Nicodemus, risking much, placed the body of Jesus in the cave tomb, without knowing the end of the Jesus story. The lives of each of these men would never be the same again. But how did it change them? Would Nicodemus still be a secret disciple?

Afterward Joseph of Arimathea, who had been a secret disciple of Jesus (because he feared the Jewish leaders), asked Pilate for permission to take down Jesus' body. When Pilate gave permission, Joseph came and took the body away. With him came Nicodemus, the man who had come to Jesus at night. He brought about seventy-five pounds of perfumed ointment made from myrrh and aloes. Following Jewish burial custom, they wrapped Jesus' body with the spices in long sheets of linen cloth. The place of crucifixion was near a garden, where there was a new tomb, never used before. John 19 v 38-41 NLT

The group of women, Jesus's mother, Mary (the wife of Clopas), and others holding their sombre, silent, vigil at the foot of the cross, waiting as they watched for the final breath of their Lord. They did not know that resurrection day was coming. And where were the disciples at this point? Were they in hiding, frightened that they too may be arrested? Were they keeping watch at a distance? What would they be thinking? But resurrection day was coming.

So now I ask myself, how will the resurrection of Jesus impact my life? How has it, how will it change my life, my thinking, my very being? Today, we declare, "It is finished." "It is paid." Christ is risen. He is risen indeed. I know that I am loved, I am forgiven, I am redeemed, I am chosen, I am a child of God, and I am special. I am family. Let this be our anthem each day.

In the Isaiah 53 passage it is so clear that the way is now open for others to experience this resurrection day. There will be many, many descendants, who will be counted free and righteous because the price for sin has been paid. It is finished.

But it was the Lord's good plan to crush Him
    and cause Him grief.
Yet when His life is made an offering for sin,
    He will have many descendants.
He will enjoy a long life,
    and the Lord's good plan will prosper in His hands.
When He sees all that is accomplished by his anguish,
    he will be satisfied.
And because of his experience,
    my righteous servant will make it possible
for many to be counted righteous,
    for He will bear all their sins.

Isaiah 53 v 10-11 NLT

An Easter Prayer

May this Easter day bring resurrection life to my heart and my home.
May renewal radiate within me and revival emanate through me.
May dawn displace the darkness and spring replace the winter in my life.
May the God of hope so fill me with joy and peace this Easter
that I may overflow with hope by His power and life forever Amen

Pete Greig Lectio 365

A Prayer of willingness to Listen by Rachel Mojo.

So often I come to you with lists and demands.
Like a tornado I spew them out as commands.
To the next task, I move on with my day
Completely missing what you might have to say.
The noise of the world clogs my ears
And clouds my mind with fog and fears.
I need you to clear my senses, O Lord!
Give me a heart in tune with your Word.
May I be ever eager to hear your voice;
May listening continually be my choice.

The I AM'S

"I am willing" Jesus

We are familiar with the great I am's of Jesus. I am the bread of life, I am the good shepherd, I am the resurrection and the life, I am the light of the world. I am the way, the truth, and the life, I am the light of the world, I am the vine. But as I am reading through Matthew's gospel, I am discovering many more I am's that are truly significant and show us the heart of Jesus.

At the beginning of Jesus' ministry, a leper approached Him, knelt before Him in worship, calling Jesus, Lord, and asked to be healed saying *"Lord, "if you are willing, you can heal me and make me clean." Without hesitation or delay, Jesus reached out and touched him. "I am willing," he said. "Be healed!"* The outward signs of leprosy may have disappeared, and the burden of being 'unclean', followed by Jesus's clear instructions as to what to do next to be accepted back into the community.

This remarkable account shows the gentle heart of Jesus. The leper would have suffered this long, progressive, isolating condition for many years. But he came to Jesus in great humility, and without demand. He knew that Jesus could heal, but would He be willing to heal him? Jesus touched the man- with the welcoming, reassuring, gentle touch of one hand to another. There was a clear and simple statement- "I am willing" as Jesus healed him with that touch. That touch was just what was needed. The man would no longer be in his isolated, lost, and broken condition where there was no mercy or pity.

When we come to Jesus with a great need we should come in humility, and with worship knowing that Jesus is able to meet that need. The leper knelt before Jesus and made no demands. He left the success or outcome of his request to Jesus. Jesus said, "I am willing."

PRAY
I can come to you Jesus, with my needs and the needs of others. I can spread them out before you, knowing that your heart is loving and

gentle. Help me to bring my requests with humility and in worship knowing that you are able.

"I am humble and gentle at heart" Jesus

Then Jesus said, "Come to me, all of you who are weary and carry heavy burdens, and I will give you rest. Take my yoke upon you. Let me teach you, because I am humble and gentle at heart, and you will find rest for your souls. Matthew 11 v 28-29 NLT

As you read these words, you see the true heart of Jesus. You see the centre of who He is, the essence of His character. Jesus is gentle and lowly, and He calls you to come to Him. Come-when you are labouring and carrying the burdens, pressures, and strains of life that you have put on yourself. Come-when you are carrying the worries, problems and demands that others may have placed upon you. Just come to Him. He is gentle, tender, welcoming, open, and willing to receive you just as you are. Just come. Come with your mess, your mistakes, your sin, your failures, your confusion, your questions, and He will receive you. Jesus is gentle and lowly at heart. His love is compassionate, tender-hearted, and merciful. He knows you and your situation inside and out. He is not harsh or heavy handed. He will not speak sharply or severely. He understands and He is gentle. So, get rid of any misconceptions and just come. As you see His heart, open your heart to Him and let Him in. Jesus is meek and lowly. He will lead gently like a shepherd, without being overbearing, placing on you high demands or being heavy handed. His burden is light, and He asks you to come to receive His rest and renewal. Come.

PRAY
Jesus, you ask me to come. You will speak gently to me. You will deal gently with me. The world is a noisy, busy place, and I might miss your voice. Help me to listen for your quiet whispers and to tune into your voice.

"Go out and stand before me on the mountain," the Lord told him. And as Elijah stood there, the Lord passed by, and a mighty windstorm hit the mountain. It was such a terrible blast that the rocks were torn loose, but the Lord was not in the wind. After the wind there was an earthquake, but the Lord was not in the earthquake. [12] And after the earthquake there was a fire, but the Lord was not in the fire. And after the fire there was the sound of a gentle whisper. **1 Kings 19 v 11-12**

"I am among you as one who serves"

Jesus's disciples had walked with Him, shared His three-year ministry, and yet had still failed to properly grasp His true heart. The disciples were in a disagreement, a dispute, about which of them might be considered the greatest. Who was the most important, who should have the higher position? Jesus gently and firmly lets them know the nature of His heart, His service, and therefore the kind of service that He would like to see in His followers. He wanted them to adjust their priorities and operate in an entirely different and perhaps alien way.

Jesus had come among them as one who serves and not as the one who was in receipt of service from others. His heart was always to meet the needs of others. He was the one willing to provide, to 'give of Himself', and to take the function or role of a servant. Jesus could not disregard or avoid the needs of the other. It was against His character to hold back from giving to those who approached Him. This is the essence and character of our Saviour. He had come among them as One who serves, and this is our Saviour still.

Do we look for recognition, attention, or reward from others for who we are or what we do? Do we compare ourselves with others? Do we want to be visible or are we happy to do whatever we do in His name, quietly in the background, unseen? It is tempting to seek a position, a platform, a title from which we can have a position of status. Like the disciples, we need to adjust our priorities and learn from the Saviour.

"Instead, the greatest among you should be like the youngest, and the one who rules like the one who serves."

As I have been thinking about these words, this old, familiar hymn came to mind.

You laid aside, Your majesty
Gave up everything for me
Suffered at the hands of those You had created
You took away my guilt and shame
When You died and rose again
Now today You reign
And heaven and earth exalt You

I really want to worship You, my Lord
You have won my heart and I am Yours
Forever and ever, I will love You
You are the only one who died for me
Gave Your life to set me free
So I lift my voice to You in adoration.

Songwriters: Noel Richards

You Laid Aside Your Majesty lyrics © Thank You Music Ltd.

In a well-furnished kitchen there are not only crystal goblets and silver platters, but waste cans and compost buckets—some containers used to serve fine meals, others to take out the garbage. Become the kind of container God can use to present any and every kind of gift to his guests for their blessing. 2 Timothy 2 v 20

"Take courage. I am here!"

And in the fourth watch between 3:00—6:00 a.m. of the night, Jesus came to them, walking on the sea. And when the disciples saw Him walking on the sea, they were terrified and said, It is a ghost! And they screamed out with fright. But instantly He spoke to them, saying, Take courage! I Am! Stop being afraid! Matthew 14 v 25-27 AMP

When you read some Biblical accounts that are very, very familiar to you, it is tempting to think that you have a full grasp of the details, the understanding, and lessons that you have received from the passage.

Then, when you read that same familiar passage in a different version of the text or a Bible commentary, your eyes are opened to something entirely new and even more significant than before. This was my experience with this well-known account of Jesus water walking towards His terrified disciples on the sea of Galilee, in the worst storm ever. The account was my next 'I am' Monday thought. "I am here." I would have reflected on the truth that Jesus is ever present, that He comes to us, and that He will reach us in any and every situation.

Then, I read the account in the Amplified version of the Bible and there was a whole new perspective. The translation of the Greek is "Take courage. I AM."

The words "I AM" relate to the account in Exodus 3 where God speaks to Moses from the burning bush and commissions him as His messenger to the children of Israel. Moses needs to know, when he speaks to the children of Israel, who can he say has sent him, what is his name, and what words shall he use?

God replied to Moses, "I am who I am". Say this to the people of Israel: I am has sent me to you." God also said to Moses, "Say this to the people of Israel: Yahweh, the God of your ancestors—the God of Abraham, the God of Isaac, and the God of Jacob—has sent me to you. This is my eternal name, my name to remember for all generations. Exodus 3 v 14-15

God reveals His Name to Moses. He is the God of their forefathers, and the God of the covenant, but He is so much more. "I Am who I AM." I am Yahweh, Jehovah. I have no equal. I exist before time itself and I will never cease to exist-I AM. I rely on nothing else for my existence-I am life itself. I AM present always. This is the One that is sending you.

So, when Jesus says to the frightened disciples in the boat- "Take courage. I AM" and calms the wind and silences the storm- then the disciples instantly know that this is no ghost. This is Yahweh, Jehovah. This is I Am. It is no wonder that the disciples worship and proclaim that Jesus is the Son of God.

And when they (Peter and Jesus) climbed into the boat, the wind died down. Then those who were in the boat worshiped him, saying, "Truly you are the Son of God." Matthew 14 v 32-33

There are other places also where Jesus refers to Himself as I AM.

Jesus replied, I assure you, most solemnly I tell you, before Abraham was born, I Am. John 8 v 58

I tell you this now before it occurs, so that when it does take place you may be persuaded and believe that I am He [Who I say I am—the Christ, the Anointed One, the Messiah]. John 13 v 19

When I fear my faith will fail
Christ will hold me fast
When the tempter would prevail
He will hold me fast
I could never keep my hold
Through life's fearful path
For my love is often cold
He must hold me fast.

He will hold me fast
He will hold me fast
For my Savior loves me so
He will hold me fast.

Songwriters: Matthew Sherman Merker

"I am there among them"

"And I tell you once more that if two of you on earth agree in asking for anything it will be granted to you by my Heavenly Father. For wherever two or three people come together in my name, I am there, right among you!" **Matthew 18 v 20 JBP**

This short passage packs a real punch. It points to the power of prayer. It points to the power of agreement when we pray together as a group, where the numbers and the size of the group are unimportant. It points to the power of community because we are called together, drawn together as His followers, and in and into His Name. It points to the fact of a relationship-a relationship with Jesus- the I Am and that with Jesus, we can talk to Him about anything and everything. It points to the fact that we can do whatever is needed to be done if it is within His purpose.

But more than any of this, it tells us that Jesus is right in the middle- He is "in the midst"-not separate or in a high up place but slap bang in the middle with us. It bases prayer within that relationship and the fact that Jesus wants us to be in relationship with Him. Although Jesus knows everything about the situation that we are in, He still wants us to talk with Him about it and it is in that prayer conversation that things may become clearer, or a new perspective gained. There is grace when we pray individually and there is grace and power when we meet with others in one place to pray.

Before the throne of God above
I have a strong and perfect plea
A great High Priest whose name is love
Whoever lives and pleads for me

Behold Him there, the risen Lamb
My perfect, spotless Righteousness
The great unchangeable I Am
The King of glory and of grace
One with Himself, I cannot die
My soul is purchased by His blood
My life is hid with Christ on high
With Christ my Savior and my God.

Songwriters: Vikki Cook / Charitie Bancroft

And the Holy Spirit helps us in our weakness. For example, we don't know what God wants us to pray for. But the Holy Spirit prays for us with groanings that cannot be expressed in words. And the Father who knows all hearts knows what the Spirit is saying, for the Spirit pleads for us believers harmony with God's own will. And we know that God causes everything to work together for the good of those who love God and are called according to his purpose for them. Romans 8 v 26-28

"I am in the Father and the Father is in me"

Jesus knew who He was. He knew where He had come from. He knew where He was going. "I am from above. I am not of this world. "He knew that He was not alone. He knew that He was with the Father and that the Father had sent Him. His words and actions were the words and actions of the Father. Jesus had made some very amazing statements about His identity, very publicly in the Temple area, during His confrontation with a very hostile group of Pharisees. Jesus had gone even further to state that anyone who looked at Him and saw what He was doing was looking at Father God. He was the I AM. To know Jesus was to know God. It is no wonder that the Pharisees were so infuriated, hostile, and angry and took up stones to stone Him. Yet, many who were listening to this dialogue and confrontation believed in Jesus.

A short while later, Jesus was preparing His disciples for the fact that He would soon be leaving them. Jesus had spoken with them about His true identity, that He was the Way, the Truth, and the Life. Philip, and the other disciples had been with Jesus throughout His ministry and yet still there were many deep things that even the disciples had not fully grasped or understood. Philip said, *"Lord, show us the Father and that will be enough for us." John 14 v 8* Jesus went on to explain that He and God, the Father were one. To see Jesus was to see God. Jesus also promised the presence of the Holy Spirit who would continue to guide and help them.

"Have I been such a long time with you," returned Jesus, *"without you really knowing me, Philip? The man who has seen me has seen the Father. How can you say, 'Show us the Father'? Do you not believe that I am in the Father and the Father is in me? The very words I say to you are not my own. It is the Father who lives in me who carries out his work through me. Do you believe me when I say that I am in the Father and the Father is in me? John 14 v 9-13*

Even though we have been walking with Jesus for many years, we may be a bit like Philip. We may still have questions about the true nature and identity of Jesus, or we may have a limited view of Him, becoming content with the small, narrow image that we have- "that will be enough for us." Let us look again at the declarations that Jesus made about Himself and be amazed and humbled.

So, Jesus said, "When you have lifted up the Son of Man on the cross, then you will understand that I am he, I do nothing on my own but say only what the Father taught me. And the one who sent me is with me— he has not deserted me. For I always do what pleases him." Then many who heard him say these things believed in him. John 8 v 28-30 NLT

PRAY
Turn your eyes upon Jesus
Look full in His wonderful face
And the things of earth will grow strangely dim
In the light of His glory and grace.

"I am sending you out"

In Matthew chapter 10, we read how Jesus sent out the twelve disciples on their first solo mission trips without Him. They are sent as Jesus's messengers, His representatives, out to local towns and villages, to announce that the Kingdom of heaven is at hand. But first, before they go public on their own, Jesus instructs the disciples on what they should expect, reassures them that the Spirit of the Father will be with them and will fully care for them, and He gives them instructions on how they should always conduct themselves.

Look, I am sending you out as sheep among wolves. So be as shrewd as snakes and harmless as doves. Matthew 10 v 16

In this first mission, the disciples would feel as vulnerable and exposed as sheep among wolves; they would need to be as shrewd, careful, and watchful as serpents; and they would need to behave without any falseness and be as innocent as doves. Sheep, serpents, and doves' paints quite a portrait of how they perhaps should behave as they go out to speak, teach, heal, and point others to the way of Jesus. But Jesus reassures them that He has prepared the way for them, and that they will be fully equipped. Although they go empty handed and are required to take no money or means of practical support, they are instructed to 'freely give'. "Freely you have received, freely give."

We too have a mission and are being sent out by Jesus. We may feel vulnerable and as insecure as those sheep. We may feel unprepared, confused, and uncertain as to the kind of reaction and welcome that we may receive. Jesus reassures us in that when we may feel tongue tied and lost then the Spirit of the Father will give us the words to say. Do not fear and do not feel alone. We are to be as wise as those serpents. We need Jesus' wisdom in how to relate and conduct ourselves with others. We need to be astute, careful, and perhaps sometimes wary, but without any hint of deceit, guile or cunning. We should do all in our power to avoid tension and conflict while we are aware that there may be opposition to our words and values. As doves, we are to be gentle, gracious, and kind, never knowingly giving offence or causing harm, but always demonstrating the compassion of Jesus in our ways and our words.

So, we are sheep, serpents, and doves. We are His representatives to those around us, presenting and representing the Saviour, the living God.

Let us go public, go out there, with the name, character, and message of Jesus.

Take my life, and let it be
Consecrated, Lord, to Thee;
Take my moments and my days,
Let them flow in ceaseless praise.

Take my hands and let them move
At the impulse of Thy love;
Take my feet and let them be
Swift and beautiful for Thee.

Frances Ridley Havergal (1836-1879)

"When I am lifted up"

The raising of Lazarus at Bethany was a major turning point in Jesus's ministry and mission, as many Jews, nobles, and religious leaders now believed in Jesus but remained silent and frightened through fear of the Pharisees, the Council, and the Sanhedrin. The Chief Priests and Sanhedrin now saw Jesus as a major threat. They feared that the Romans, would regard the 'Jesus movement' as an insurrection and would therefore suppress and destroy the Jewish way of life, their temple, holy place, city, and civil organisation. Caiaphas, the High Priest for that year, prophesied that it was better for one man to die for the people than for this to happen. From this point on the Sanhedrin plotted to have both Jesus, and Lazarus killed. Jesus no longer appeared publicly among the Jews but travelled to stay with His friends at Bethany as Passover was approaching.

Jesus knew that the time of His death was near, and He knew the manner of that death-an horrific, Roman crucifixion.

"And when I am lifted up on the cross, I will draw everyone to me." He said this to indicate how he was going to die. John 12 v 32-33 TLB

Jesus would be lifted up on the cross but then He would also be lifted up into heaven after His resurrection-His mission then complete. It is amazing that such a cruel death should attract and draw out so much love from His followers. Jesus' death on that cross, far from repelling people or turning people away, was the one thing that would attract, pull in, call people to approach and to come near. *"And I, as I am lifted up from the earth, will attract everyone to me and gather them around me." He put it this way to show how he was going to be put to death.* John 12 v 32-33 MSG

It was that very death that dealt with our sin, separation, and judgement. *"He cancelled the record of the charges against us and took it away by nailing it to the cross. In this way, he disarmed the spiritual rulers and authorities. He shamed them publicly by his victory over them on the cross".* Colossians 2 v 14-15 NLT

So, give yourselves humbly to God. Resist the devil and he will flee from you. And when you draw close to God, God will draw close to you.
James 4 v 7-8 TLB

It is the love and sacrifice of Jesus that is so attractive and which 'draws' us towards Him. Jesus continues to draw others to Him by the strength of this pure love and offer of forgiveness.

SONG Living Hope by Brian Johnson & Phil Wickham

Who could imagine so great a mercy?
What heart could fathom such boundless grace?
The God of ages stepped down from glory
To wear my sin and bear my shame
The cross has spoken, I am forgiven
The king of kings calls me His own
Beautiful saviour, I'm yours forever
Jesus Christ, my living hope.

Songwriters: Brian Johnson / Phil Wickham

Living Hope lyrics © Be Essential Songs, Bethel Music Publishing

"I am going to prepare a place for you"

At the Passover meal, Jesus shared some very disturbing facts with His disciples- one of them would betray Him, He would soon leave them, and they would not be able to follow, and to Peter, that he would betray Him three times. The disciples would face some shocking, distressing events over the next few hours and days, and it is in this context that Jesus tells them not to be troubled, distressed, or anxious but that He was going away to prepare a place for them.

"You must not let yourselves be distressed—you must hold on to your faith in God and to your faith in me. There are many rooms in my Father's House. If there were not, should I have told you that I am going to prepare a place for you? It is true that I am going away to prepare a place for you, but it is just as true that I am coming again to welcome you into my own

home, so that you may be where I am. You know where I am going, and you know the road I am going to take." John 14 v 1-4 JBP

When the family come together again at Christmas, Easter or a special occasion, the preparations go into overdrive. The bed shuffle is completed, bathrooms cleaned, futons, bed settee and extra mattresses are in place, so that everyone has a bed to sleep in even if they might not have their own room. The extra shopping and cooking are done, meals and emergency backup meals are in hand, and the freezer is crammed. We are preparing for the family to come home. Is everything ready? Have we forgotten anything?

Jesus was going to prepare a special place, dwelling places, for His disciples and He was speaking of heaven, His Father's house. Jesus says to the disciples and to us, that there are many mansions or rooms and that these dwelling places will be our permanent home. And the best news ever is that He has gone to prepare for us- to make it ready, and that He will be there to receive us when the time is right. The preparations are complete, the sacrifice has been paid, and He has gone home to His Father. The even better news is that one day we will be with Jesus-permanently. He will welcome us home -to His home.

I have just discovered this amazing song by Casting Crowns. It may be helpful for anyone who has lost someone very close to them.

SONG: Scars in Heaven by Casting Crowns - (Official Music Video)

https://www.youtube.com/watch?v=qCdevloDE6E

*The only scars in Heaven, they won't belong to me and you
There'll be no such thing as broken, and all the old will be made new
And the thought that makes me smile now, even as the tears fall down,
Is that the only scars in Heaven are on the hands that hold you now.*

Songwriters: John Mark Hall / Matthew Joseph West

Scars in Heaven lyrics © Anthem Entertainment Lp, Sony/ATV Music Publishing LLC

"I am leaving you with a gift"

"I am leaving you with a gift—peace of mind and heart. And the peace I give is a gift the world cannot give. So don't be troubled or afraid." John 14 v 27 NLT

Jesus is preparing the disciples for the tragedies that will soon unfold and reassures them with the promise of an incredible gift. This gift to them and to us is the profound peace of heart and peace of mind. This incomparable peace, cannot be spoiled, interrupted, or disturbed by any external factors. This peace is not just an absence of trouble, tension, worry, or conflict and it is always available coming from a deep relationship with Jesus. This gift cannot be found anywhere else.

The thing about gifts is that we must accept, receive them and be thankful. Sometimes we may be offered a gift that might seem to be less desirable, not to our taste or it may be a duplicate of something that we already have. The Christmas season is notorious for people panicking about appropriate gifts to give to family members and friends. At this time of year, we resort to gift vouchers or socks.

Thankfully our heavenly Father knows exactly what we need. His gifts are freely available to us and will always be the perfect, exact thing for us. His gifts are tailor made, personalized, just the right thing and are well timed into the bargain. He gives His peace of heart and mind but sadly, so often we fail to see His open, generous hand and so we struggle on in our own strength trying to work things out and use our own resources. His peace is incomparable- there is nothing else like it and it cannot be manufactured in any other way. Other methods of stress relief, relaxation techniques, mindfulness and the like may have their place but there is nothing that can beat the gift of God's peace to us.

The peace of God is much greater than the human mind can understand. This peace will keep your hearts and minds through Christ Jesus. Philippians 4 v 7 NLT

Don't fret or worry. Instead of worrying, pray. Let petitions and praises shape your worries into prayers, letting God know your concerns. Before you know it, a sense of God's wholeness, everything coming together for good, will come and settle you down. It's wonderful what happens when Christ displaces worry at the centre of your life. *Philippians 4 v 7 MSG*

PRAY-Collect of the Church of England
Almighty God,
from whom all thoughts of truth and peace proceed:
kindle, we pray, in the hearts of all, the true love of peace
and guide with your pure and peaceable wisdom
those who take counsel for the nations of the earth
that in tranquillity your kingdom may go forward,
till the earth is filled with the knowledge of your love;
through Jesus Christ your Son our Lord,
who is alive and reigns with you,
in the unity of the Holy Spirit,
one God, now and for ever.

"I am in you"

I am in my Father, and you are in me, and I am in you. John 14 v 20 NIV

As Jesus continued to prepare the disciples for His departure, and calm their fears, He promised the gift of the Holy Spirit-another Helper who would be with them so that they were never alone. The Holy Spirit would be their helper, comforter, strengthener, mediator, and teacher who would stay with them always. The Holy Spirit would continue to draw them into their relationship with Jesus and with God the Father. He would bring all things to their remembrance and continue to show them Jesus even though they would not be able to see Jesus in the flesh. It would be an ongoing life of relationship with God the Father, Jesus the Son, and the Holy Spirit. A very clear introduction to the Trinity. This gift would be at the request of Jesus to the Father. Jesus will ask the Father to send the Holy Spirit to them and the Father would send the Spirit in His 'Name.' For us too this is a unique relationship- we are 'in' Jesus, Jesus is 'in us' and because Jesus is 'in' the Father then we are included in this close bond with Him. The Helper, the Holy Spirit, will be given to us at the request of the Son, so that like the early disciples, we are never alone. He will continually signpost us to Jesus, empower us, and be our intercessor, and comforter. The Message version of the Bible calls the Holy Spirit, 'The Friend.'

I'm telling you these things while I'm still living with you. The Friend, the Holy Spirit whom the Father will send at my request, will make everything plain to you. He will remind you of all the things I have told you. I'm leaving you well and whole. That's my parting gift to you. Peace. I don't leave you the way you're used to being left—feeling abandoned, bereft. So don't be upset. Don't be distraught. John 14 v 25-27 MSG

Let us celebrate the fact that we are in Christ. Pray too for those people who feel bereft, isolated, disconnected, fearful, and broken that they may know that the Comforter, the Friend, the Helper, and the Strengthener is nearby.

Gracious Spirit, dwell with me—
I myself would gracious be,
And with words that help and heal
Would Thy life in mine reveal;
And with actions bold and meek
Would for Christ my Savior speak.

Truthful Spirit, dwell with me—
I myself would truthful be
And with wisdom kind and clear
Let Thy life in mine appear;
And with actions brotherly
Speak my Lord's sincerity.

Words: Thomas T. Lynch, 1818-1871

"I am the Alpha and the Omega"

And the one sitting on the throne said, "Look, I am making everything new!" And then he said to me, "Write this down, for what I tell you is trustworthy and true." 6 And he also said, "It is finished! I am the Alpha and the Omega—the Beginning and the End. To all who are thirsty I will give freely from the springs of the water of life. Revelation 21 v 6-7 NLT

"I am the Resurrection and the Life"

The Dragonfly

There is a fictional story entitled *Water Bugs and Dragonflies*; a book written by Doris Stickney. Water Bugs and Dragonflies is a beautiful modern parable about transformation, that explores the challenging topic of death and loss that even young children can access and may find helpful.

The story begins with a colony of water bugs who spend their lives at the bottom of the pond, although occasionally one of these strange looking creatures, would climb out of the pond, up the stalk of a water lily, disappear, and never come back. The water bugs are curious to know what happens to each friend, why they leave and where they go. So, the water bugs promise each other that the next water bug that climbs out of the pond must return and tell the others what happens to them above the surface of the pond.

The next water bug to leave the pond, discovers that a startling change has occurred to his body, that he has grown four beautiful wings and a tail, and that he is able to fly freely in the air and the sunshine. He has become a dragonfly. Moving his beautiful silver wings, he finds himself flying above the pond where his friends the water bugs live. Then he remembers the promise that he made while he was still a water bug at the bottom of the pond.

The dragonfly attempts to return through the water surface of the pond but realises that with his changed body he cannot return to the pond, the water, and his friends. The beautiful dragonfly also realizes that even if he could go back, not one of the water bugs would recognize him and know him in this new, changed body. He would have to wait until they become dragonflies too and join him beyond the water of the pond.

This is a picture of what happens to us at the change to our old bodies, and of passing on to a new life in heaven with Jesus. It is impossible to go back and to explain to others what the new life is like. A transformation has taken place.

The Wilderness

From the wilderness to the valleys

Observe the commands of the Lord your God, walking in obedience to him and revering him. For the Lord your God is bringing you into a good land—a land with brooks, streams, and deep springs gushing out into the valleys and hills. Deuteronomy 8 v 6-7 NIV

The Israelites were on the edge of entering God's promised land and Moses was reminding them of the forty-year journey through the wilderness and its purpose. The wilderness lessons were to teach them concerning God's leading, His promises, His provision, and His testing "to prove your character, and to find out whether or not you would obey his commands." From the barren, challenging wilderness God would bring them into a land of brooks, streams, springs, and rivers that were gushing with life giving water. *"For the Lord your God has blessed you in everything you have done. He has watched your every step through this great wilderness. During these forty years, the Lord your God has been with you, and you have lacked nothing." Moses, Deuteronomy 2 v 7 NLT*

Taking the land was too big a task for them-on their own. It was beyond their ability, and they would be facing impossible odds-the people, the fortifications, and the cities. God was asking for them to acknowledge their dependence on Him, to be teachable, not to over-estimate their own abilities, plans, and skills, and to constantly listen to Him and His guidance. When facing the seemingly impossible task before them they were to acknowledge *"that man does not live on bread alone but on every word that comes from the mouth of the Lord." Deuteronomy 8 v 3*

We may often be in a wilderness time of testing, and it can be excruciating, confusing, debilitating, and painful. We may face seemingly insurmountable obstacles and problems with no clear solution or path. But we hang on to the assurance that 'God has been with us these forty years' and that He will bring us from barrenness to blessing, to a place of gushing springs and flowing water. From confusion, uncertainty, and wilderness wandering, God will lead us into His prosperity and provision. We are His beloved.

Beloved Is Where We Begin Jan Richardson, janrichardson.com

If you would enter into the wilderness,
do not begin without a blessing.

Do not leave without hearing
who you are: Beloved, named by the One
who has travelled this path before you.

Do not go without letting it echo in your ears,
and if you find it is hard to let it into your heart,
do not despair. That is what this journey is for.

Trusting in the wilderness challenges

At each point in their journey across the wilderness, new challenges appeared for the Israelites and their hearts failed them. They murmured, doubted, complained, found fault, raised angry voices, and looked back to what they had left behind. Yet at Shur, Marah, Elim, Rephidim, and Horeb, God was faithful and always made new provision. Their journey through the wilderness and the challenges that they would have to face as they took the land were going to be great. But God's presence was with them in the cloud and the fire, they had renewed their covenant, and He continually reassured them of His purpose and keeping.

"Remember not the former things,
nor consider the things of old.
Behold, I am doing a new thing;
now it springs forth, do you not perceive it?
I will make a way in the wilderness
and rivers in the desert.
The wild beasts will honour me,
the jackals and the ostriches,
for I give water in the wilderness,
rivers in the desert,
to give drink to my chosen people,
the people whom I formed for myself
that they might declare my praise. Isaiah 43 v 18-21

When we go through very tough times- and Jesus never promised us that things would be easy or straightforward, - then we need to have confidence in God's presence, purpose, and love for us. It is so easy to grumble, moan, become bitter, blame, store up a catalogue of wrongs, and wallow in self-pity. We need the Holy Spirit to continually bring us back into the loving heart of God and to realign ourselves with Jesus in heart, mind, and soul. God did not abandon His people, the Israelites, and He will not abandon us. God was creating a new people, doing a new thing, making a new way, giving new resources, and throwing a praise party. He gives water in the wilderness.

A Lent Reflection. (*Author unknown*):

Fast from worry; feast on trusting God.
Fast from complaining; feast on appreciation.
Fast from hostility; feast on tenderness.
Fast from unrelenting pressures; feast on unceasing prayer.
Fast from judging others; feast on Christ dwelling in them.
Fast from discontent; feast on gratitude.
Fast from anger; feast on patience.
Fast from pessimism; feast on optimism.

Fast from bitterness; feast on forgiveness.

Fast from self-concern; feast on compassion for others.

Fast from discouragement; feast on hope.

Fast from things that depress; feast on truths that uplift.

Fast from suspicion; feast on truth.

Fast from gossip; feast on purposeful silence.

Fast from problems that overwhelm; feast on prayer that sustains.

Fast from thoughts that weaken; feast on promises that inspire.

Fast from apparent darkness; feast on the reality of light.

The Way through the Wilderness

We have been reading several books and daily guides written by Bear Grylls, who is one of the world's most recognised adventurers. He is a former Special Forces soldier and Everest mountaineer. He has experienced some of the harshest environments on earth in all four corners of the globe, which have taught him some valuable life lessons. His writings are inspirational. Phil, Sam, and I have been working our way through his daily devotional books, A Survival Guide for Life, Soul Fuel, and now Mind Fuel which identifies the ways to build mental resilience. Bear Grylls knows that life in the wild can teach invaluable lessons but that extreme situations and any kind of wilderness, forces an individual or group to face up to fears, dangers, and challenges. When you are entering any kind of wilderness, it can be terrifying.

The children of Israel had travelled to the edge of the unknown, the wilderness. But God was with them, guiding them by His presence, directing their steps, giving them light, by cloud and fire. *"God went* ahead of them in a Pillar of Cloud during the day to guide them on the way, and at night in a Pillar of Fire to give them light; thus, they could travel both day and night. The Pillar of Cloud by day and the Pillar of Fire by night never left the people." Exodus 13 v 21 MSG

"Because of your great compassion you did not abandon them in the wilderness. By day the pillar of cloud did not fail to guide them on their path, nor the pillar of fire by night to shine on the way they were to take. You gave your good Spirit to instruct them. Nehemiah 12 v 19-20

God's guiding presence and light never left them. Although I am not sure that I would have wanted to travel through the wilderness at night. Moses, Bezalel, Ohaliab, and the host of skilled crafts people had built the Tabernacle, the Tent of Meeting, and it was here that God would continue to be present and to meet with Moses and the people. "Whenever the people saw the pillar of cloud standing at the entrance to the tent, they all stood and worshipped, each at the entrance to their tent. The Lord would speak to Moses' face to face, as one speaks to a friend. Exodus 33 v 11

God's loving guiding presence was always there. When the cloud settled over the Tent of meeting, the people stayed still. When the cloud lifted, this was the indication to move and to go forward. It was a clear system of Stop-Go.

Then the cloud covered the Tabernacle, and the glory of the Lord filled the Tabernacle. Moses could no longer enter the Tabernacle because the cloud had settled down over it, and the glory of the Lord filled the Tabernacle. Now whenever the cloud lifted from the Tabernacle, the people of Israel would set out on their journey, following it. But if the cloud did not rise, they remained where they were until it lifted. The cloud of the Lord hovered over the Tabernacle during the day, and at night fire glowed inside the cloud so the whole family of Israel could see it. This continued throughout all their journeys. Exodus 40 v 34-38

PRAY
Lord, I need to be reminded of your continual presence. Help me to be sensitive to your presence with me and to your guiding voice. May I know

when to stop, and remain, and when to go and to move forward. May I wait for you to show me the right path.

Your ears will hear a word behind you, "This is the way, walk in it," whenever you turn to the right or to the left. Isaiah 30 v 21 AMP

This is what the Lord says: "Stand at the crossroads and look; ask for the ancient paths, ask where the good way is, and walk in it, and you will find rest for your souls. Jeremiah 6 v 16 NIV

The bronze snake in the wilderness

And as Moses lifted up the bronze snake on a pole in the wilderness, so the Son of Man must be lifted up, so that everyone who believes in him will have eternal life. For this is how God loved the world: He gave His one and only Son, so that everyone who believes in him will not perish but have eternal life. John 3 v 14-16 NLT

Moses and the Israelites had travelled on and were now on the threshold of their promised land but were forced to take a long detour around the land of Edom. This setback, the hardships, and the sheer length of their journey, meant that the people were discouraged, exhausted, and dispirited. This time, they did not just complain about Moses, but they turned their anger, frustration, and words against God. "Why have you brought us out of Egypt to die here in the wilderness?" they complained. "There is nothing to eat here and nothing to drink. And we hate this horrible manna!" God had faithfully provided manna, the bread of heaven, each day for them, and yet now they called it 'this worthless bread.'-So, God sent poisonous serpents among the camp and many people were bitten and died. But God also provided the remedy for their desperate situation. The people confessed their sin against God and against Moses, and asked Moses to pray for them. Moses was instructed to make a bronze serpent and to place it on a pole and those who looked at the serpent recovered and lived. They just had to look and live. Their sin was dealt with. The remedy was sure. They didn't have to do anything else. No potion, balm, ointment, or medicine would be effective. All that was required was to look and live. *Numbers 21 v 4-9 NLT*

In John's gospel we read that Jesus was in conversation with Nicodemus, a Pharisee, a significant ruler of the Jews and teacher of the Law, a member of the Sanhedrin, and a man of status and authority who had come to Jesus at night. Jesus talked with him about the kingdom of God, new birth by water and the Spirit, eternal life, and the Son of Man who must be 'lifted up.' Nicodemus, confused and amazed at the words, failed to grasp the depths of Jesus's meaning. Jesus then strikingly connected His words of salvation with the account of Moses and the bronze serpent lifted up in the wilderness. Nicodemus would know this story well. We understand Jesus's words to be a clear message about His crucifixion and death. Jesus would be lifted up on the cross and then later also lifted up to heaven. These words, this message announce that God loved, God gave, God welcomes, and God's salvation is for all who will look to Jesus. Simply come and look. The bronze serpent made by Moses was a picture of Messiah, the Son of Man, and God's remedy for sin and judgement. Accepting Jesus at the cross is the only remedy for sin. Our choice is look to Him, see His finished work, and believe. Nothing else will work. No action on our part, no good works, no effort is needed- but simply to look, to love and to trust.

Hymn: Author: Cecil Frances Alexander 1818-95

There is a green hill far away outside a city wall,
where our dear Lord was crucified, who died to save us all.

We may not know, we cannot tell what pains he had to bear,
but we believe it was for us he hung and suffered there.

He died that we might be forgiven, he died to make us good.
That we might go at last to heaven, saved by his precious blood.

There was no other good enough to pay the price of sin.
He, only, could unlock the gate of heaven – and let us in.

Lord Jesus, dearly have you loved, and we must love you too, and trust in your redeeming blood and learn to follow you.

The Project Management Coordinator

Come, all of you who are gifted craftsmen. Construct everything that the Lord has commanded. Exodus 35 v 10 NLT

We are having major building work done at home, with two new bathrooms being redesigned and remade-at the same time. Four weeks into these eight-week projects we are thinking that we are slightly crazy! These are large projects that you would normally undertake when you have a generous amount of time and energy. However, we are using Paul, a Project Management Coordinator, whose skills and experience we know and trust, who is both an amazing designer and project coordinator. But our normal routines are disrupted by two plumbers, one electrician and his apprentice, one tiler, two plasterers, a garage full of their essential equipment and tools, and the hardware for two new bathrooms, and a whole heap of disruption and dust.

Paul is the overseer of all. He designed, planned, budgeted, produced schedules of work, finance statements and invoices, purchased all the hardware, organized timelines, ensured resources were available when needed, problem solved and adapted, communicated with each trade's person, and kept all running timely, smoothly and to plan. He is director extraordinaire, problem solver, communicator, and the backbone of the project. He knows his team and directs them well.

This experience encouraged me to look back to the account in Exodus in which God gave very precise instructions to Moses concerning the building of the new Tabernacle and its furnishings. The most skilled workers and artisans of many different crafts were needed to accomplish the task. Overseeing the work were two individuals, Bezalel and Aholiab. These two men were the project coordinators of the work, who were Spirit filled, highly skilled, gifted with wisdom, ability, and expertise in all kinds of crafts and able to teach their skills to others.

"The Lord has filled Bezalel with the Spirit of God, giving him great wisdom, ability, and expertise in all kinds of crafts. He is a master craftsman, expert in working with gold, silver, and bronze. He is skilled in engraving and mounting gemstones and in carving wood. He is a master at every craft. And the Lord has given both him and Oholiab son of Ahisamach, of the tribe of Dan, the ability to teach their skills to others. The Lord has given them special skills as engravers, designers, embroiderers in blue, purple, and scarlet thread on fine linen cloth, and weavers. They excel as craftsmen and as designers." Exodus 35

They also needed the skilled craftsmen and women, a gifted workforce of workers in wood, bronze, gold, embroidery, gemstones, skins, spinning, sewing, and much more, to work together to achieve God's perfect design. God has chosen us uniquely to be part of the work for Him and He has gifted each person with something unique and valuable. May God help us to see and to encourage those gifts in others. We are His workforce and part of His new Tabernacle and Temple. Overarching all of this is our Sovereign Lord and His perfect plan.

In his grace, God has given us different gifts for doing certain things well. Romans 12 v 6
So, you are no longer outsiders or aliens, but fellow-citizens with every other Christian—you belong now to the household of God. Firmly beneath you in the foundation, God's messengers and prophets, the actual foundation-stone being Jesus Christ himself. In him each separate piece of building, properly fitting into its neighbour, grows together into a temple consecrated to God. You are all part of this building in which God himself lives by his spirit. Ephesians 2 v 21 JBP

PRAY the prayer of St Ignatius Loyola:Teach us, good Lord, To serve thee as thou deservest;
To give and not to count the cost; To fight and not to heed the wounds; To toil and not for seek for rest; To labour and not to ask for any reward Save that of knowing that we do thy will.

Esther

Banquets and Celebrations

Phil and I have made many trips to China and one of the Important Chinese customs is to welcome guests on the night of their arrival with a special banquet. This is a very important meal, often formal, where dignitaries, local officials, and staff are invited to attend. It is a time for the exchange of gifts and words of welcome. There is always too much food and during and after the meal, there are toasts with alcohol, words of praise and commendation, and for our Chinese friends, the opportunity to enjoy too much alcohol and merriment. These banquets are often followed by a late-night karaoke session with even more riotous humour, singing, and laughter. The welcome to guests, the gifts, the food, drinking, celebrations and fun, reminds me of the forthcoming celebration of Purim. Purim is the time for fun and feasting for Jewish families, with dressing up costumes, masquerades, the giving gifts, and offerings to the poor all added to the mix.

Purim is celebrated on the 14th of March, when our Jewish neighbours and friends, and Jewish people around the world will celebrate the festival. We learn about the origins of Purim in the Book of Esther, when victory against an enemy, Haman, with his plans to annihilate the Jewish race in the 127 provinces of King Ahasuerus, across what is now Persia, was won through the wisdom, cooperation, trust, fasting and prayer, of two people, Mordecai and Esther and the quiet but unseen presence of God. It tells of the victory of the Jews against a possible massacre. The festival is one of the most loved and joyous of Jewish holidays, celebrations and perhaps the high point in their calendar. There is plenty of food, the drinking of alcohol, mainly wine, the giving of gifts of food to friends, family and neighbours, and gifts to the poor. Another popular custom is the dressing up in costumes on Purim, perhaps as a reminder that Esther and Mordecai concealed their Jewish heritage at the King's court.

In the Book of Esther there are so many extravagant banquets! In the third year of his reign, Ahasuerus gave a banquet for all his nobles, officials, princes, and military leaders lasting 6 months. Then, the king gave a banquet, lasting seven days, for those from 'the least to the greatest' living in the capital, Susa. Queen Vashti gave a banquet for the palace women. When Esther was chosen to replace Queen Vashti, "the king gave a great banquet, Esther's banquet", displaying his affluence. He proclaimed a holiday throughout the provinces and distributed gifts with "royal liberality." Esther gave two banquets, but only for the king and Haman alone, part of her plan to shame the wicked Haman and point to the truth about his plans. When Haman had finally been punished, Mordecai promoted to second in command, and the Jews no longer threatened, there were more celebrations. "In every province and in every city to which the edict of the king came, Esther's Decree, there was joy and gladness among the Jews, with feasting and celebrating. And many people of other nationalities became Jews because fear of the Jews had seized them."

So, the feast of Purim is celebrated every year as *"the time when the Jews got relief from their enemies, and as the month when their sorrow was turned into joy and their mourning into a day of celebration. He (Mordecai) wrote to them to observe the days as days of feasting and joy and giving presents of food to one another and gifts to the poor." Esther 9 V 22 NIV.* There is a time for celebrations, friends and family meals, anniversaries, weddings and banquets, laughter and games, and putting on the 'glad rags.'

When the righteous see God in action they'll laugh, they'll sing, they'll laugh and sing for joy. Sing hymns to God; all heaven, sing out; clear the way for the coming of Cloud-Rider. Enjoy God, cheer when you see him! Psalm 68 v 3 The Message

PRAY: Give me joy in my heart keep me praising.

From Obscurity to Queen

As we read through the Book of Esther we detect and feel the hand of God working, even though His name is never mentioned in the text. God's presence and involvement in the lives and characters of Mordecai and Esther, and in their roles leading to the rescue of the Jewish people, are clearly perceived. Esther, an orphan, had been adopted by Mordecai. 'Mordecai had a cousin named Hadassah, whom he had brought up because she had neither father nor mother. This young woman, who was also known as Esther, had a lovely figure and was beautiful. Mordecai had taken her as his own daughter when her father and mother died.' Esther 2 v 7 NLT Esther was Jewish, not Persian, and therefore had no rightful claims to be considered for what was to be her new role as the Queen of Persia. But the hand of God was with her. After the demise of Queen Vashti, and the decree to find a new queen for King Ahasuerus, Esther was selected to join the young women in the protected harem, as a potential candidate. This might not have been her first choice of career but a clear purpose and plan for her life was slowly working its way out. God was putting her in a position to save her nation.

One person can make a difference! We witness Esther's courage and faith. We witness her willingness to act and to risk her own life. We see her patience in undergoing the twelve months of preparation under the guidance of Hegai, with the careful following of his advice before she is even presented to the king. Her patience, wisdom and integrity, together with her acceptance of advice from Hegai and Mordecai at every step, would lead to the salvation of the Jewish people from a marked destruction. Before Esther goes before the king to plead for her people, she asks Mordecai to arrange for a three day fast and prayer among her people and only then does she act.

Mordecai reminds her that her role and request are so significant, that she may have come to the palace "for such a time as this." *"For if you remain silent at this time, relief and deliverance for the Jews will arise from another place, but you and your father's family will perish. And who knows but that you have come to your royal position for such a time as this?" Esther 4 v 14.* Mordecai's position at court also changed, becoming *" second in rank to King Ahasuerus, preeminent among the Jews, and held in high esteem by his many fellow Jews, because he worked for the good of his people and spoke up for the welfare of all the Jews." Esther 10 v 3.* Mordecai had worked faithfully behind the scenes-watchful, patient, and without self-promotion and because of this selfless, outward care and concern, was promoted to high office.

The decree concerning the liberation of the Jews became known as "Esther's Decree," and the new festival of Purim was established. "These days should be remembered and observed in every generation by every family, and in every province and in every city. And these days of Purim should never fail to be celebrated by the Jews—nor should the memory of these days die out among their descendants." Esther 9 v 28

In the account of Esther, we witness the overarching love and plan of God for His chosen people, for their survival, the preservation of their identity, and in addition, non-Jews turning to the Jewish faith because of all that they have witnessed.

Questions:

Do I trust God's plan for my life?
Do I feel inadequate because of my circumstances, my family, my education?
Can I follow advice?
Can I work behind the scenes, unnoticed?
Can I wait patiently?
Can I work for the care and concern of others?

Joshua

Stones of Remembering

Past- Present -and Future.

Joshua and the Israelites had left their camp at Acacia Grove (love that title) and had moved to the edge of the Jordan River ready to cross into God's Promised Land. Joshua had declared to the people, "today, you will know that the Living God is among you." God would miraculously stop the waters of the Jordan to allow the Israelites to cross in the same way that He had intervened at the Red Sea. When the river flow had been stopped and the people had crossed over, Joshua instructed men to collect large stone boulders from the middle of the dry riverbed and to construct two large memorials of stone- one in the middle of the river itself and one at their first camp at Gilgal, their gateway to the Land of Promise. These stone memorials were to be tangible, physical reminders and symbols of what God had accomplished on their behalf and signposts to future generations of God's saving power for their present and their future. When future generations asked, "What do these stones mean?" they could explain and declare how God had saved His people *"so that all the peoples of the earth might know that the hand of the Lord is powerful and so that you might always fear the Lord your God." Joshua 4 v 22-24*

But Joshua gave instructions for stones to be placed in a memorial mound in the middle of the riverbed even though the river waters would flow back to cover them. This memorial mound was equally significant. But why were they there when for most of the time they would be covered and unseen? This would seem to be a very strange thing to do.

Joshua also set up another pile of twelve stones in the middle of the Jordan, at the place where the priests who carried the Ark of the Covenant were standing. And they are there to this day. *Joshua 4 v 10*

The mound of stones on the riverbed would be visible again when the water level was low or when there was a drought in the land. It seemed to me that in dark times- and there would be dark times of challenge and battle as they occupied the Land of Promise-God was giving them a reminder of His presence, promise, and power.

As God had been with them in the past, He would be with them in their struggles and their future. Gilgal, with its mound of stones on land and in the river itself, was to become a secure base for Joshua and his armies, to which they could always return, and so this special place with its memorial stones would remind them of God's powerful intervention.

As God had been with them in the past, He would be with them in the challenges of future battles. Their first conflict at Jericho was not far away. The stones would speak to their children, their children's children and all the people of the earth of God's love for His people- He is with you.

Perhaps we all need our Gilgal stones. We need these markers, signposts, memorials, memories of the high places when God has stepped into our lives.

PRAY:
Father God, remind me of my Gilgal places. Those times when you have been close and have moved in my life-and especially when times are tough, and I don't know what I am doing.

From Vulnerability to Victory

But the Lord said to Joshua, "Jericho and its king and all its mighty warriors are already defeated, for I have given them to you! Joshua 6 v 2 TLB

The Israelites camped at Gilgal, their entry point to the promised land and it was here that the men were circumcised, the camp celebrated Passover, renewing their covenant with God, and for the first time, ate of the fruit and crops of Canaan. The daily delivery of manna ceased, and they now tasted the goodness of what was to be their new homeland.

But Gilgal was in full sight of the stronghold city of Jericho which made them very vulnerable to attack as they had to remain in camp for many days until the men were healed. Joshua was met by the Commander of the Lord's Army, an Angelic being or Jesus Himself, and was given precise instructions about battle plans and the complete capture and consecration of Jericho, and its inhabitants. The battle plan seemed crazy, improbable, illogical, risky, but their victory was assured. The defeat of Jericho is a familiar story.

Following the Ark of the Covenant the people marched round Jericho's city walls in complete silence, one circuit each day for six days, and then on the seventh day seven times around the city. Then finally, they would be given the signal to shout. "Shout!" for the Lord has given you the town. But while they were walking round the city, again they would be in a very vulnerable position- 'sitting ducks' as some people might say. But they were "in the presence of the Lord, "in His sight, and He had promised that the city would be given over to them. So, no matter how vulnerable, and exposed they might feel, how much they might complain 'well this doesn't make much sense,' their God was with them. The battle had already been won.

We often find ourselves in very perplexing, confusing, and vulnerable situations. Things do not seem to make any sense, and we cannot see a clear way forward. We fail to see where God is in our situation and circumstances, and although we move forward, we do so with some trepidation. But trust in God as He knows the end from the beginning and the bit in between.

With your hand you drove out the nations, and planted our ancestors; you crushed the peoples, and made our ancestors flourish. It was not by their sword that they won the land, nor did their arm bring them victory; it was your right hand, your arm, and the light of your face, for you loved them. Psalm 44 v 2-3 NIV

For the Lord takes delight in his people; he crowns the humble with victory. Psalm 149 v 4 NIV

But thanks be to God! He gives us the victory through our Lord Jesus Christ. 1 Corinthians 15 v 57

PRAY
I often feel fragile, confused, vulnerable, and wavering on the edge. Jesus, you know what I am feeling. You alone know what I can bear. You will protect, strengthen, and encourage and bring me into that better place.

Moving on from Failure

Then the Lord said to Joshua, "Do not be afraid or discouraged."
Joshua 9 v 1

After the victory at Jericho, Joshua sent his forces to capture the city of Ai- but they were defeated and humiliated by their failure to take the city. Their failure at Ai was because of the sin of Achan who had taken trophies and spoils of war for himself ("I saw a beautiful robe from Babylon, 200 silver coins, and a bar of gold weighing more than a pound, wanted them so much that I took them.") Joshua and the elders were rightly distraught at the failure and were unable to move forward. They were immobilised. Joshua and the elders put their faces in the dust of the ground, and were prostrate with dismay before the Ark, the presence of God. But God said to Joshua, "Get up! Why are you lying on your face like this? In a sense, why are you here? This failure is not the end. Deal with the cause of the failure, get your face out of the dirt, get up and move on.

When the cause of their defeat was dealt with, then the Lord said to Joshua, "Do not be afraid or discouraged. Take all your fighting men and attack Ai, for I have given you the king of Ai, his people, his town, and his land." God did not just give Joshua the encouragement that he needed to get up and go forward, He gave him a very specific battle plan which involved a clever deception and the ambush of their enemies. Joshua followed the plan to the letter and victory was given.

God's words were 'do not fear', do not be discouraged. Do not let fear or failure hold you back. Do not give into fear but act despite the fear.

Joshua not only needed to have courage for himself, but he needed to inspire courage in the camp.

We may sometimes feel that we have messed up big time. We have made a colossal mistake, caused deep offence, committed a sin that has affected others, caused a major rift or breakdown in relationships, and may feel that we cannot go forward. We are stuck in that moment of time. We have failed and our failure has caused damage. But our loving Heavenly Father says, 'get up-do not be disheartened, crushed, and discouraged-get up and go. 'Do not be afraid because I am with you.

After the victory at Ai, Joshua built yet another pile of unhewn stones. But this time the stones were an altar on which burnt offerings and peace offerings were offered, as Moses had instructed, and the whole camp renewed their covenant with God.

Come as you are

Come out of sadness
From wherever you've been
Come broken hearted
Let rescue begin
Come find your mercy
Oh sinner come kneel
Earth has no sorrow
That heaven can't heal
Earth has no sorrow
That heaven can't heal.

So, lay down your burdens
Lay down your shame
All who are broken
Lift up your face
Oh wanderer come home
You're not too far
So lay down your hurt
Lay down your heart
Come as you are.

There's hope for the hopeless
And all those who've strayed
Come sit at the table
Come taste the grace
There's rest for the weary
Rest that endures
Earth has no sorrow
That heaven can't cure.

Fall in his arms
Come as you are
There's joy for the morning
Oh sinner be still
Earth has no sorrow
That heaven can't heal
Earth has no sorrow
That heaven can't heal.
Songwriters: Ben Glover / David Crowder / Matt Maher;
https://www.youtube.com/watch?v=adSTiuAnbls

A Broken Connection -Deception

On Thursday night we had a power cut at The Barn. The engineer who responded to the emergency call out discovered that the main power line to our house, but to no one else in the street, had become completely corroded and the connection had failed. This has led to a major repair and renewal of the supply, requiring the digging up of our front grassed area and a part of the road. We were without power for a few hours and have been left with a huge mess of a hole in the ground which will need to be filled in and restored. The broken power connection at night affected was challenging and had implications for the stored food in our fridge and freezers. We were without power and there were consequences and challenges.

As I have continued reading in the Book of Joshua, I read in chapter nine, a situation where Joshua and the leaders of the Israelites lost their power connection with the Lord and did not consult Him about the matter of the Gibeonites. Consequently, they were tricked and deceived into making an alliance with them, and an oath which they could not break. The Gibeonites had pretended that they had travelled from far distant lands and therefore were not occupants of the land of Canaan. However, in reality, they occupied three towns within three days of travel from Joshua and his camp. Had this been discovered, the Gibeonites as with all the other thirty-one kings and kingdoms in Canaan, would have been subjugated or killed.

So, the Israelites examined their food, but they did not consult the Lord. Then Joshua made a peace treaty with them and guaranteed their safety, and the leaders of the community ratified their agreement with a binding oath. Joshua 9 v 14-15 NLT

The people of Israel grumbled against their leaders because of the treaty. But the leaders replied, "Since we have sworn an oath in the presence of the Lord, the God of Israel, we cannot touch them. Joshua 9 v 19

The consequence of their failure to seek out God's will led to an unwanted agreement, a compromise, with grumbling and complaints from their people. Joshua and the leaders were tricked, deceived, and seduced into believing the envoys from Gibeon. They had failed to pray and use their God given wisdom. There were uncomfortable consequences to this failure.

We too can rush on and not stop to pray, consider carefully, and use our God given wisdom at a crucial turning point. Let us not lose our power line connection.

A Promise Kept with Integrity

Joshua and the Israelites had captured the central area of Canaan, dividing the country into two halves, with its separate kingdoms and thirty-one kings. It was surely now a case of divide and conquer the whole of the land. The Israelites were ready and in a prime position. Joshua and the leaders had been duped by the Gibeonites into making an agreement, an oath, and an alliance with the Israelites- but a promise was a promise. He had taken an oath with the Gibeonites for their safety and protection, and he could not break a promise under any circumstances. He was a man of integrity and faithfulness.

However, Joshua's next challenge came hard on the heels of this when the five southern kings of Canaan, under the military guidance of the king of Jerusalem, gathered their armies together to fight against the Gibeonites- the very group that had come under the protection of Joshua. So, the Gibeonites sent a message to Joshua at the tents at Gilgal, saying, "*Do not leave your servants alone. Hurry and help us. Joshua 10 v 6*

Now this could have presented Joshua with a quandary. If he did nothing, did not respond to the cry for help, and Gibeon was taken by the enemy armies of the southern kings, then Joshua would be relieved of his problem. He could turn a blind eye and the problem might go away. The unwelcome alliance would have been dealt with and terminated. But Joshua could not allow that to happen. An oath, a promise, an alliance must be kept and upheld as a matter of integrity. He could not turn his back on the vow with the Gibeonites. But Joshua did not just keep his promise, he kept it with energy and commitment sending his best soldiers from Gilgal to defend them. This involved a march of eight to ten hours, travelling twenty miles in the black of night to avoid detection, and finishing off with a steep uphill climb before the final attack. *So, Joshua went up from Gilgal. He took with him all the men of war and all the strong soldiers. The Lord said to Joshua, "Do not be afraid of them. For I have given them into your hands. Not one of them will stand in front of you." So, Joshua came upon them by surprise by traveling all night from Gilgal. Joshua 10 v 7-9*

God had promised to be with them. God would go on to demonstrate His power and hurl huge hailstones at the enemy armies. Joshua and his men had done all that they could do and then God stepped in and did what only He can do. The victory was complete.

Joshua had the qualities of integrity, faithfulness and being a man of his word. He could have taken the easy option but did not. A lesser man may have ignored the cry for help. He could not. Joshua had kept his promise. God then kept His promise of a complete deliverance -in a miraculous way.

PRAY
Help me to be a person of integrity whose word can be trusted. When it might be easy to take a convenient way out, help me to be true to my word.

Boundaries

As we go into a new academic year, it is perhaps good for us to reflect on the importance of the healthy boundaries that we may need to establish and keep for ourselves, in terms of activities, commitments and our emotional. physical and mental wellbeing. Our lives and days can often become frenetic and over busy, leaving little space for physical and emotional recovery, so it may be helpful to review these activities and pressure points at this point, so that we can avoid feeling over stretched and overwhelmed in the future.

As I continue to read the Book of Joshua, the children of Israel have continued to occupy and possess the Promised Land. Joshua then describes in microscopic detail how each of the twelve tribes were to be allocated specific geographical areas of territory, with very clear demarcations and boundaries. These areas with their boundary lines were described and recorded in so much detail so that there could be no confusion later. Every hill, mountain, river, pastureland, water hole, valley and town were clearly outlined and allocated.

God had given to Joshua very specific instructions about the lands that were taken and those that were still to be possessed and included. *"Include all this territory as Israel's possession when you divide this land among the nine tribes and the half-tribe of Manasseh. Half the tribe of Manasseh and the tribes of Reuben and Gad had already received their grants of land on the east side of the Jordan, for Moses, the servant of the Lord had previously assigned this land to them. Joshua 12 v 7-9*

Clear cut boundaries are not just helpful- they are essential. We need to know where our limits and boundaries are and so do other people. If we do not have clear and precise boundaries, then things often tend to drift and before too long we will find that we are tired and stressed. I am speaking to myself at this point! So, before everything starts up again, review your boundary lines, with the gracious wisdom and help of the Holy Spirit. And no matter how great the demands, -take time to rest and replenish. Jesus took time to come to one side and to rest and to be with His Father. He would go into the hills and perhaps re charge His physical, mental, and emotional resources.

So, the Lord gave to Israel all the land he had sworn to give their ancestors, and they took possession of it and settled there. And the Lord gave them rest on every side, just as he had solemnly promised their ancestors. None of their enemies could stand against them, for the Lord helped them conquer all their enemies. Not a single one of all the good promises the Lord given to the family of Israel was left unfulfilled; everything he had spoken came true. Joshua 21 v 43-45

PRAY: Lord, there is much to do and land to be taken but you have promised to be with us, and your promises do not fail. Help us to work and walk at your pace-not too fast and not too slow, not running on ahead and not looking back.

Promises fulfilled

So, the Lord gave to Israel all the land he had sworn to give their ancestors, and they took possession of it and settled there. And the Lord gave them rest on every side, just as he had solemnly promised their

ancestors. None of their enemies could stand against them, for the Lord helped them conquer all their enemies. Not a single one of all the good promises the Lord had given to the family of Israel was left unfulfilled; everything he had spoken came true. *Joshua 21 v 43-45 NLT*

Then Joshua summoned the Reubenites, the Gadites and the half-tribe of Manasseh and said to them, now that the Lord your God has given them rest as he promised, return to your homes in the land that Moses the servant of the Lord gave you on the other side of the Jordan. But be very careful to keep the commandment and the law that Moses the servant of the Lord gave you: to love the Lord your God, to walk in obedience to him, to keep his commands, to hold fast to him and to serve him with all your heart and with all your soul."

"The Lord has driven out before you great and powerful nations; to this day no one has been able to withstand you. One of you routs a thousand, because the Lord your God fights for you, just as he promised. So be very careful to love the Lord your God. *Joshua 23 V 9-10*

So, Joshua took the entire land, just as the Lord had directed Moses, and he gave it as an inheritance to Israel according to their tribal divisions. Then the land had rest from war. *Joshua 11 v23*

Leadership

designed by © freepik.com

Israel served the Lord throughout the lifetime of Joshua and of the elders who outlived him and who had experienced everything the Lord had done for Israel. *But then: the People of Israel dispersed, each man heading back to his own tribe and clan, each to his own plot of land. At that time there was no king in Israel. People did whatever they felt like doing. Judges 21 v 24-25*

I worked as a teacher for twenty-seven years, with the schools where I was employed being almost entirely in the tough, inner-city areas of Leeds. My most consistent spell of teaching in one school, was in a Gipton school, Leeds for eight years. The Headteacher was an amazing person and leader who we loved, respected greatly, and worked alongside with gratitude and commitment. There were many challenging issues for the staff to contend with, but she led the team with wisdom, compassion, and we benefitted from her considerable years of experience with the families in this area of Leeds. She knew what she was about, and we had her consistent support. When she retired, she was replaced by a string of acting headteachers who had little experience with this kind of school. After three or four successive acting executive headteachers, issues began to appear quite quickly both with staffing, parents, and pupils. Staff looked for other opportunities or left teaching altogether, pupil behaviour deteriorated, and things began to spiral downwards remarkably quickly. Even the enticement of an inflated salary for a new headteacher did not attract anyone of the same calibre as the original head who had served for many, many years. The experience taught me that good leadership is key and that we should value and support our leaders.

Joshua and Caleb were the leaders who had first entered the Promised Land. They had been strong leaders and lived long lives of service. Joshua lived to the grand age of 110 years and Caleb eighty-five years of age. During Joshua's lifetime, the Israelites had faithfully followed his lead and had been faithful to their God being witnesses to everything that the Lord had done. But after the death of Joshua, things would change as they entered their new settled existence in the land. There was no leader or leadership. New generations had little memory of Joshua and the exploits that he had directed under God and so they drifted away from the covenant and the promises that had been made to their God at Shechem.

*Israel served the Lord throughout the lifetime of Joshua and of the elders who outlived him and who had experienced everything the Lord had done for Israel. Joshua 25 v 15 But then: ""The People of Israel dispersed, each man heading back to his own tribe and clan, each to his own plot of land. At that time there was no king in Israel. People did whatever they felt like doing." **Judges 21 v 24-25**

What followed were repeated periods of time when the Israelites were defeated and broken, but then returning in desperation to their God, who was always faithful to them. Then, after experiencing God's mercy and intervention through the judges, Deborah, Gideon and Samson, they would forget their gracious God again to become a defeated people crying out for help once more. It was a constant cycle.

Pray for our leaders.

Dear brothers and sisters, honour those who are your leaders in the Lord's work. They work hard among you and give you spiritual guidance. Show them great respect and wholehearted love because of their work. And live peacefully with each other. I Thessalonians 5 v 12-13 Paul

PRAY
for wise and discerning hearts, and the energy and strength that they need. That they will have God's heart and His wisdom and honour God in all their decisions. Give them patience, grace, and perseverance. Give us grace as we follow. Amen

Encounters

Strengthened to serve: Simon Peter's Mother-in-Law

Simon's mother-in-law was bedridden, sick with a high fever, so the first thing they did was to tell Jesus about her. He walked up to her bedside, gently took her hand, and raised her up! Her fever disappeared and she began to serve them. Later in the day, just after the Sabbath ended at sunset, the people kept bringing to Jesus all who were sick and tormented by demons, until the whole village was crowded around the house. Jesus healed many who were sick with various diseases and cast out many demons. Mark 1 v 29-32 TPT

No sooner had the fever left than she was up fixing dinner for them. MSG

I live in Capernaum and love and support my daughter and her husband, a Galilean fisherman. Times are hard and their income is uncertain. He is a good man, he works hard, and endures impossible hardships to make a living, selling the fish in the market that he and his brother catch. Fishing on the Sea of Galilee is a treacherous and demanding business and there are the boats and nets to manage. The dramatic changes in the weather on the water make the fisherman's life and work even harder. Their life together is challenging. For all his faults- which in my opinion are many, Simon is strong, hardworking, and a good and faithful man. He may not be the most stable of characters as he can be strong willed, impulsive, and doesn't always think through his plans. He is full of ideas, schemes, and crazy notions, tends to speak before thinking, and often fails to consider the impact of his words on others. But I love him dearly and I do what I can to help them both.

Recently, his time has been taken up with other things. The two brothers have met with a local itinerant teacher who visits the towns and villages. By report, this man has been doing some amazing things. I hear accounts of Him healing ailments and diseases. But more than that, He brings a message of love and transformation which is certainly different to what you might hear in our local synagogue. I am intrigued by this man and have heard Andrew and Simon give Him high praise. They are keen to follow Him. But what of my daughter? If they go off to the countryside, leaving boat, net, and livelihood behind, what will become of her?

One day, I began to feel very unwell, and my sickness turned to a high fever. I was unable to carry on with any daily chores, and unable to help my daughter. I became so ill that I had to take to my bed. I could take no food and my condition was growing worse. Barely opening my eyes, I felt a gentle touch on my hand. It was the teacher who had been calling the men to leave their nets and to follow. His touch and His voice were gentle. The strangest of things happened next. I immediately felt the fever go from my body and my energy return. How could this be? From being so sick and laid up in my bed, I was restored, energized, renewed. I got up out of the bed, washed and dressed and immediately thought that food should be prepared for our guests. Then, later in the day, after Sabbath, our little house was surrounded by other visitors- many visitors, dozens of visitors! It seemed as if the whole village was descending on our little home. They came with various illnesses and Jesus began to heal them, one by one. They were healed, restored, and freed.

I was restored and renewed, and I had a place to serve the One who had touched my life.

Thoughts

We have trusted in Christ and received His free grace and salvation. But we are also saved to serve- not in our strength but with His strength and power. We are strengthened to serve.

As you live this new life, we pray that you will be strengthened from God's boundless resources, so that you will find yourselves able to pass through any experience and endure it with courage. Colossians 1v 11

I pray that out of his glorious riches he may strengthen you with power through his Spirit in your inner being, so that Christ may dwell in your hearts through faith. And I pray that you, being rooted and established in love, may have power, together with all the Lord's holy people, to grasp how wide and long and high and deep is the love of Christ, and to know this love that surpasses knowledge—that you may be filled to the measure of all the fullness of God. Ephesians 3 v 16-19

A Roadblock Situation: The Rich Young Ruler
Matthew 19 v 16-30

I am from a privileged family. I have always known security, received a sound, quality education and a good religious upbringing. I have been taught to be morally upright, to do the right thing, to follow the teachings of the scriptures and the Pharisees. I have followed the commandments to the letter and the instructions of the Teachers and the Rabbis at the synagogue. I have learned well, so that now I am one of the youngest leaders, joining those of senior years, who are teaching others in the ways of God. I have conformed to the rules, maintained high standards of behaviour, and earned the respect of all in the community. I am set for high things, but I am not at peace. Why do I feel so dissatisfied? There is a discontent in my soul, a void that I cannot fill and for all my superior moral behaviour and high standards there is something lacking. I have learned and followed the Pharisaic rules from early childhood. I am a conformer of the first order so why do I feel so empty?

I heard of this young, untrained itinerant Teacher whom many are following and was eager to find out the secret to His ministry, success and following. I sought Him out in good faith, coming before Him respectfully, open minded, with a genuine need to learn, being aware of the void in my life. I needed to ask Him- what particular thing do I need to do in order to have eternal life? I have followed all of the rules and commandments and so what one, good thing do I need to do now? Have I done enough for a reward in heaven? Is there a guarantee of my place in the eternal? I will do whatever is required.

His answer was straightforward and shocking. I was to sell all I had and follow Him. He had discerned that my strongest, my hearts attachment, was to my wealth, status, position, and privilege. He was asking me to relinquish the control of my life to Him and to simply follow. He had read my heart. I now saw that eternal life is not by 'doing' but by 'being'.

I was cut to the core. His words had penetrated deep and caused immense conflict. To say that I was troubled was an understatement. This was too much to ask. How could it be that my high moral life would count for nothing in the new kingdom? My heart was heavy and with great sorrow I quietly turned away from Him, returning to the privilege of my wealth and the security of all that was familiar.

Thoughts

This rich young ruler had hit a roadblock, a crossroads and he could go no further until he had relinquished the control of his life to the One who was calling him to follow. There was a hindrance, an obstacle that prevented him from moving forwards. He had stalled and could not move forward to his desired path of knowing his place in the kingdom of God. So, he was immobilized, stifled, and frustrated. A breakthrough would not come easily now.

There is one significant and perhaps life changing sentence in this account of the rich young ruler.

And Jesus looking upon him loved him, and said to him Mark 10 v 21

Perhaps if he had continued in conversation with Jesus, he may have begun to see things from a new perspective. He may have realized that he could not begin do this by himself and that Jesus would not ask Him to do it on his own. When the disciples asked Jesus to explain the challenge of riches to them, Jesus gave a simple, clarification- trust God to help you.

The disciples were staggered. "Then who has any chance at all?" Jesus looked hard at them and said, "No chance at all if you think you can pull it off yourself. Every chance in the world if you trust God to do it." MSG

We may each face some turning point, a blockage on our journey of faith, something that we are holding onto, or some unexpected challenge. He does not expect us to do this on our own. His grace and power to change us, is sufficient. We can't pull it off by ourselves. We need to keep reminding ourselves of this.

This wonderful hymn was written by Frederick William Faber. (1814-1863):

There's a wideness in God's mercy, like the wideness of the sea;
there's a kindness in His justice which is more than liberty.

There is no place where earth's sorrows
are more keenly felt than heaven:
there is no place where earth's failings
have such gracious judgement given.

For the love of God is broader than the measure of man's mind;
and the heart of the Eternal is most wonderfully kind.
But we make His love too narrow, By false limits of our own.
And we magnify His strictness, With a zeal He will not own.

If our love were but more simple, we should take Him at his word;
And our lives be filled with gladness from the presence of the Lord.

Crumbs under the table: Matthew 15 v 22-28

My daughter is ill. My emotions are raw, I am empty, drained of energy, physically exhausted with no help and no place to turn to. It has been this way for years. There is no respite and no hope. I have prayed to the God of Heaven, and the God of the Jews, but He is deaf to my cries. My neighbours now avoid me as they too feel helpless, without comfort or kind words, overwhelmed by my needs. They will do no more.

I hear rumours of one Jewish Teacher who is gentle, merciful and who heals. There are rumours that He has travelled to Tyre and Sidon, into our Gentile area, but that He is lying low. Why would He come if He does not want to be seen? Why is He here at all? We are Canaanites, with ancient hostilities between us and the Jewish nation. We are Gentiles, outsiders, of mixed nationalities and so why would He come here?

My heart is racing. I must find this teacher healer. If the reports are true, then He is my only hope. I am Greek, born in Syrian Phoenicia and so what am I to Him? I have no position or claim on Him, no status or privilege that He should even speak to me. I am no insider. I am a foreigner, an outsider. Yet I will go.

I came down from the hills and found Him out in His place of rest and retreat as He sat with His followers. I dared to approach. The words startled even me as they came out of my mouth. "Lord, Son of David, have mercy on me and heal my daughter." There was only silence and the strange looks of those who were with him. Silence. A painful silence. I told my story, shared my pain and pleaded but there was only silence. I was turned away by the followers, but I continued to plead my case, my daughter's needs, her need for healing, my hope. They grew frustrated, angry with me, forceful, unkind even. "Send her away, or take care of the woman, she's driving us crazy, she won't go, she's calling after us, following us" they called to the Master.

I came back to the healer and dropped to my knees at his feet. My words were simple. "Master, help me". His gaze touched my heart and my soul, but His words were few. "I was sent to the lost sheep of Israel. It is not right to take the bread out of the children's mouths and throw it to the dogs." I sensed what He was saying – what He meant. He was the Jewish Jesus, the Messiah. My reply came quickly. "But the little dogs eat the scraps from the children's hands and that fall from the master's table." There was a change, a smile, and a gentle response. "Woman, you have great faith. Your request is granted."

My faith, my confidence in Him and His power was the turning point. He had put hurdles in my way to prove and test my heart. My daughter was healed at that very moment. I knew it. Few words needed to be spoken. I returned home and everything was different.

But here is the strange thing. He left our region and went back to Galilee. I heard that there was a miracle involving bread and fish among thousands. What a strange affair. He gave bread to the hungry by their thousands. But I had been given a crumb, a morsel of bread and that was enough. I was changed.

But she came and bowed down before him and said, "Lord, help me!"

She knew that she had no rightful claim to His grace, but she asked and kept asking.

"Ask and it will be given to you; seek and you will find; knock and the door will be opened to you". Matthew 7 v 7

Pray
Jesus, you seek out those in need. Your grace reaches out beyond borders, boundaries, and groups.   Help us to see others-all others- as you see them. To see them as those who need of your love and care irrespective of nationality, status, or cultural group.   Broaden our vision.

Bent Double: Luke 13 v 10-17

I see feet and not faces. It has been this way for as long as I can remember. I look down at the dirt, the stone path, the mud, the dirty feet, and sandals of those who pass me by. I do not look up to the trees, the birds, the sky, the window, the doorway, or the eyes of those who pass me by. I am unseen though a familiar presence, a non-person, nameless, insignificant and of no value. My world is small. Every simple task poses new challenges of pain and inconvenience. I cannot lift, I cannot carry, I cannot reach up high and I cannot contribute. I am invisible yet a target of children's jokes and laughter. I am humiliated, sorrowful, ashamed, a burden to others and the burden of my shame and weakness has been with me for most of my life-for eighteen whole years. I shuffle silently into the synagogue each Sabbath and hide with the women at the back. I do not want to be seen. My hiding is almost complete as I stand among the flowing robes and scarves.

But I am seen. There was One whose grace and compassion saw me in my hiding place though I could not hope to see His face. I was called forward. It was an invitation that I could not avoid. There was a stunned silence as I was guided to the front to where the gentle voice had called me. I had no expectation, no understanding of what might happen, or desire to meet this new teacher. I was in the familiar place, the safe place- hidden in plain sight. His words came as a shock. "Woman you are set free." There was no pre-amble, exchange of introductions, announcement to the gathered or the synagogue leader. Those simple words only and a gentle touch. And I was released. How it happened I cannot say. I only know that my back grew stronger, my weakened and limp muscles were renewed and for the first time I could stand tall. I was straight and I could see faces. Those faces changed and there was a surge of joy, praise to God, gasps of wonder and for the first time in many years I opened my mouth and I publicly praised and glorified God for my release.

The synagogue leader was not pleased. I could see his scowl of disapproval and dismay. For the first time I could read the faces of others. And for the first time I saw His face, the face of Jesus. I was no longer the nameless one, the ignored, the cripple but I was now 'the daughter of Abraham'. I was significant, valued, part of a community with a contribution to offer. I was changed. But I was not the only one who was changed. The whole synagogue erupted with praise and thanks. I was released, set free, rescued, and redeemed. I can never forget that day. But there were others there that day who were also released.

Pray
Jesus you are all compassion.
I want to fall into your grace, compassion, and mercy all over again.
You see me. You call me. You set me free. How can I not praise you?

The alabaster jar: Luke 7 v 36-50

The alabaster jar has been sitting on the shelf for as long as I can remember. Just sitting there, unopened, gathering the dust of years. I can barely look at it. The jar is meant to be so full of promise- a gift from a parent to a child to be given to the new husband and broken at his feet as an act of commitment, honour, and devotion. But I have no need of such a gift or promise. There is no one who would consider me as a bride.

My hopes are unfulfilled, wasted, as the jar sits there accusing me, as I have given myself to so many different men. I have lost count of the number of men who have used and abused me. I do not know their names and I am now nameless and ashamed, my entitlement to marriage gone. But the jar of precious perfume, the oil that should be poured out as an act of extravagant love, sits there still.

I heard that a new teacher had arrived in town. It was said that He was a friend of tax collectors and sinners, that He loved the un-loveable, that He touched the untouchable, that He could heal, and that He could forgive sin. My sin lays heavily upon me and burdens my soul and my very being. The weight of it is crushing me. Could this teacher lift the weight of my guilt and sin and set me free? I was no longer afraid of those who judged, accused, tormented, hurt, and spat at me in the street. I would walk past them and their taunts and find this Jesus. I would pass their doors and windows and seek the mercy of the One who says that He can forgive and redeem.

But how can I enter the house of the Pharisee? I have met with so much rejection that it is an old friend to me. so, I will not knock at the door to be turned away. I have decided. I will take my precious jar, the one thing that I have, and enter secretly, quietly, unnoticed. My one thing I will give to Him, pouring out the precious oil from the jar, as my act of love. I am nothing. So, I entered the room secretly, hiding my face and settled at the feet of the prophet, the One on whom all my hopes were laid as He reclined at table. My heart was bursting with emotion- my overwhelming need, my longing for forgiveness and relief, my love and devotion for the one who could turn my life around. And so, my scarf falls away and as my tears fall freely, I wash His feet, dry them with my hair and pour out the precious perfume on His feet. The room is filled with the perfume but also the angry silence of the onlookers and the Pharisee. He says nothing. He does nothing. They are all stunned by the sight before them.

The horrified silence is broken by the gentle words of the teacher Himself. He spoke to the Pharisee. "Simon, I have something to say to you". A story of forgiveness followed, a story of two debtors, one who owed little and one who owed a great deal. Both were relieved of their debt and released. Then a gentle rebuke to the Pharisee. "You gave me no warm greeting, water for my feet, or oil for my head and yet this woman has not failed to wash and kiss my feet and anoint them with oil." He knew me. He had seen my need and my love, my silent pleading and repentance, and gave His forgiveness and His peace. I will remember His words until my dying day. "Your sins are forgiven." "Your faith has saved you, go in peace." Those words are written on my heart.

My precious alabaster jar with its perfume is gone- but so is my sin.

The Pharisee had seen my lifestyle, my notoriety and my many sins. He had not seen me. The teacher had seen my heart, my sorrow, my desperate need for change, and my longing for a new way of love. He had found me. I left that place in peace.

Pray
Lord, I am in that place again. Thank you that on the cross you cried out, "It is finished." I ask for your forgiveness again. I can live in your grace.

A frantic search: Luke 2 v 41-45

I cannot forget that dreadful time. How can you lose a child? My mind still reels from the memory of those days, and I feel again that dreadful mix of emotions- guilt, horror, despair, anger, frustration, desperate anxiety, trauma, and the nagging question-how could he do that to me, to us. How could I do that to him? How do you lose a child? But that time was a turning point for me.

We had been making the journey for as long as I can remember. It was our twelfth year of journeying to Jerusalem for Passover. I am an old hand at the preparation, packing and organising for the trip. The preparation starts well before we even get to Festival. It is getting easier now as the children are a little older. It was so hard when I had a baby to manage. Can you imagine being away from home for a two-week trip? We travel twenty miles each day before stopping to camp overnight and as Jerusalem is sixty miles from Nazareth, the journey alone takes three or four days before we reach the city. The last part of the journey is the hardest as we climb the hills towards Jerusalem. Then the festival celebrations follow, before the arduous journey back again. We are weary and longing for home by the time we have finished. Every year I worry about the cost of such a journey and whether we need to do this every year. But we are faithful and loyal to the Jewish requirements.

But that year's Passover journey will be etched in my mind forever! We had had made our journey and had celebrated Passover, enjoying time with family, friends, and the acquaintances with whom we had travelled over so many years. Jesus and the other children had played happily along the route there and new friends had been made. On our return journey we were preoccupied with the packing and moving and as we travelled from the city, had not noticed that the boy was not with us. We imagined that he was with one of our other family groups or with friends travelling in our large caravan as we made our way back to Nazareth. But by the end of that first day of travel I could not find my child. How does a mother do that? How do you overlook your child in the busyness and activity of a journey? Our frantic search was futile and so we returned to Jerusalem. Another desperate day of travel and painful worry. By now two days had gone. I could not sleep or eat. By the third day we were in Jerusalem and searching all the places that were familiar to us and where a child may go. Then at last we found him- and it was not where we expected him to be.

He was sitting in the Temple with the scholars and teachers, asking questions and joining their discussions. I was joyful, relieved, and angry all at the same time. "Why have you done this to us? Your father and I have been out of our minds looking for you" were my first words. I was frantic with worry. His reply was short and simple. "Didn't you know that I must be in My Father's house?" Then I began to see more clearly. Through my tears of relief, I began to see the Man and not the child. I reached back into the secret stores of my mind for the words of promise for the child- my child, but not just my child. I held these things dearly, deep within myself. These thoughts were my secret treasure store of truths that I had sadly overlooked in the ordinariness and routine of life. We returned quietly, occasionally silently, to Nazareth. I watched my child mature, grow strong in body and spirit, being blessed by God, and admired by those who knew Him.

In the child I now had seen the man, the Son of Man, the promised teacher, and saviour, the one that we were hoping for.

Thoughts

In the routine, the busyness, the ordinary, the stuff of daily life, and the demands we can lose sight of Jesus. We lose Him. He was there and then He was not. Maybe we have been walking this way for years and we have failed to turn and look for Him while we keep on walking.

A costly Compassion: The Good Samaritan
Luke 10

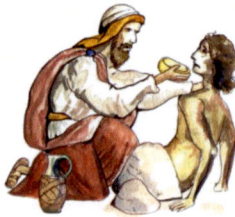

Perhaps I was foolish for being a solitary traveller on that mountain road, but my journey was urgent. The attack, when it happened was brutal, shocking and I lost everything that I had including my clothing. I was left for dead with no means of identification, little chance of discovery or help. Although barely conscious I was aware of two people who had passed on the road without stopping. I was frightened for my life, fearing that it would end here, battered, abandoned and alone. But then my rescue came and from someone who would be regarded as my enemy, the 'other', the outcast, the infidel, the foreigner and the despised one. It was life-saving compassion. He had no regard for my 'otherness', my tribe, status, religious connection, or observance. He dealt with my wounds and made plans for my care. The Injured

When I saw the tangled mess of flesh and blood how could I turn away and not stop to help? Here was a desperate man struggling with injuries that could cause his death. His identity, status, racial group became irrelevant. At that point, he became my neighbour, my family, my brother- a relationship not defined by any normal boundaries - but by his sheer need. I had the means to help him. The risk to my own life on that road was hopefully small. I knew the road, the Inn, and I had the means to help. The Inn keeper knew that I am a man of my word and that I would be good for the money when I next returned. My heart stirred and action followed. The Rescuer

Thoughts

The Samaritan offered a costly compassion. He could have acted out of fear and so taken no action but to move along, considering his own safety. But he did not act out of fear. He acted out of compassion for 'the other'. It was scary, involved physical effort and energy, was financially costly, took initiative, planning, promises and assurances.

"Who is my neighbour?" My neighbour may be one to whom I would least expect to be a neighbour. Jesus changed the question round completely to "what does a neighbour do?" Jesus showed a very clear picture of what a neighbour does. His final words are "Go and do likewise" further reinforcing the message "Do this and you will live". May we never act out of fear but always out of love.

When Jesus saw the crowds, he had compassion for them, because they were harassed and helpless, like sheep without a shepherd. Matthew 9 v 36

Martha and Lazarus: I am the resurrection

I cannot begin to describe the range of conditions and emotions that I experienced- exhaustion, despair, grief, loss, confusion, anger, shock, joy, and elation. Our brother had died and been restored to us. How can I explain such an event?

We had nursed our brother for many days and had sent word to Jesus asking Him to come to us quickly. Every day that had passed we had hoped that Jesus would come. When death finally came to our home, we were overwhelmed with grief. It was with very heavy hearts that the burial went ahead without our dear friend Jesus and his followers. Then I received word that Jesus was on His way to Bethany and so leaving my sister with the gathered mourners at home, I hurriedly went out to the edge of the village to meet with Jesus. In my distress, words burst from my mouth- "My Lord, if only you had come sooner, my brother would not have died." The words sounded accusatory, hostile almost with an element of blame. The weariness of the whole period of mourning had taken its toll on me and so my words were perhaps harsh. Checking the tone of my words I added "but I know that if you ask God for anything, he will do it for you." What was I saying? What was I hoping for?

His gentle reply followed. "Your brother will rise and live." My hope was only of resurrection on the final resurrection day, an event that was sometime in the future and yet the impact of His words seemed to point to something different. "Martha", Jesus said, "You don't have to wait until then. I am the Resurrection, and I am Life Eternal. Anyone who clings to me in faith, even though he dies, will live forever. And the one who lives by believing in me will never die. Do you believe this?" My words flowed quickly and easily. "Yes, Lord," I replied, "I believe that you are the Messiah, the Son of God, who is to come into the world." In that moment I knew that all would be well.

I hurriedly returned to Bethany, to our house of grief, mourning and loss, but with a new sense of expectation and hope. I quietly and discretely called for my sister to follow me, as the Teacher had arrived at the edge of the village and was calling for her. In her haste and eagerness, she aroused the interest and concern of the gathered mourners and comforters, who immediately followed us, thinking that we were heading for the tomb. On reaching Jesus, our common grief touched our friend deeply as we wept at our shared loss. Together we journeyed to the tomb, a simple cave with a stone laid across the entrance. There were those in the group who followed who muttered and questioned the Teacher's care and commitment to our family. "Could not He who opened the eyes of the blind man have kept this man from dying?"

Then His words stunned and shocked. "Take away the stone from the tomb". I hoped to intervene, quietly stating the obvious to our loving friend, saying that any odour from the tom would be distressing. But He was in control, His words powerful, announcing that we would see the glory of God in this moment, His manner firm yet gentle. He prayed to His Father in heaven and then called out to our brother, "Lazarus, come out!" All eyes were on that cave entrance as Lazarus stumbled and shuffled out of his cold tomb. Then in gentle tones Jesus instructed the men to remove the strips of linen cloth and grave clothes and to set him free. And now Lazarus was truly free. We had seen it with our own eyes.

I cannot tell you of the emotions that I went through in those moments. Tears flowed freely- tears of confusion, release, joy- a range of feelings for which there are no words. Many of our friends and fellow mourners now came to believe in Jesus, the healer, the Teacher, the Messiah.

I am Martha- a single woman from an insignificant village on the outskirts of Jerusalem and yet it was to me that Jesus declared those profound words that I can never forget. "I am the resurrection and the life." I am Martha, the village girl, the practical, the organized, the hard worker, the girl at home, and yet from me Jesus had drawn from deep within my soul, words of faith and trust, and an understanding of true resurrection. Resurrection is not an event in some future time, but resurrection is a Person.

Jesus said to her, "I am the resurrection and the life. Those who believe in me will live, even though they die; and those who live and believe in me will never die."

Pray

When you are at your lowest point, Jesus is not absent. He sees, He knows, and He will come. When you need His presence the most, He will come, with perfect timing, bringing His peace and words of grace. When all seems to be lost, and without life, He will bring His life.

I can see clearly: Bartimaeus

Bartimaeus of Jericho

I live in Jericho. I spend my days sitting by the roadside, unable to work or provide for myself. It is lonely by the roadside, but I have learned to listen carefully, to read the mood of passers-by and to know if they will help or ignore the blind man begging at their feet. I have learned to listen to the crowds, to the children with their games, to the mothers scolding or singing to their children. I have also heard tales of the Teacher Jesus, the Jesus of Nazareth who people called the son of David and who they hope will be the One to save Israel.

I will never forget the day it happened. On that day there would be a breakthrough in my life that I could never have thought possible. Let me tell you how it happened. I was begging by the roadside as usual when I heard the noise of a very large crowd. Someone shouted across to me that it was Jesus of Nazareth and His followers on their way out of the city. So, I started to shout out for help. "Son of David, have mercy on me!" I got louder and louder. "Son of David, have mercy on me!" The crowd tried to shut me up. They told me to stop, to leave the roadside. They would have kicked me into silence if they could have. But I shouted even more and called out even more loudly. I would not be silenced. I would not be rebuked or held back.

He had such a gentle voice. I heard Him say "Call him." He had heard my cries and called for me. I was helped up to my feet and throwing off my cloak I was directed into the presence of Jesus. "What do you want me to do for you?" He asked. My words were brief. "Rabbi, I want to see." He simply said, "Go, your faith has saved you."

It was instant, dramatic, life changing. I saw the crowd. I saw the face of Jesus, the Teacher, the One who had healed me and at that moment I made the decision to leave everything and to follow Him.

The man of Bethsaida

I live in Bethsaida. One thing that you should know about me is that I am blind and so I depend on others to lead and to help. One day, news spread in the town, with great excitement, that Jesus, the healer was travelling through with His disciples. He had been this way before and so His reputation had gone before Him. The news was now out there and could not be silenced. My friends had heard of this Jesus and were determined to get me to Him. "Surely He will heal you" they said, "as He has healed others". So, they almost dragged me out of my home, leading me hurriedly to the Healer. They brought me before Him and pleaded with Him, begged Him, urging Him to consider my situation and to show mercy and to heal. What happened next was strange beyond words.

The Healer gently took hold of my arm and carefully led me out of the town to a quiet place, away from prying eyes. I am used to this kind of help, but His hand, His touch was different- gentle, sensitive, loving. What happened next was even stranger, almost bizarre and totally unexpected- a shock really. I was aware of Him spitting on my eyes and gently touching

215

them. Then He asked me "do you see anything?" Things at first seemed to be blurred, unclear, hazy and indistinct. Once again, He touched my eyes and as I looked intently into the far distance I could see clearly, perfectly and the realization of what had just happened began to dawn on me. I could see men. I could see clearly. And I could see Jesus. But the strangeness continued as He told me not to go straight back to town. "Do not enter the village," He said. I believe that He did not want me to immediately broadcast what had just happened to me. But surely within days the news would spread? How could I keep this quiet?

Thoughts

It was after this event that Jesus took His disciples to one side and asked them some very significant and searching questions. "Who do people say I am?" and then "Who do you say I am?" Jesus. I believe that He was asking them to deeply consider what kind of Christ they thought Him to be. What was their understanding of Jesus as Saviour or Messiah, and could they understand the nature of the suffering that He would encounter?

Often, I lose sight of Jesus. I don't have my eyes fixed on Him. Quite often my vision is blurred, out of focus or just short sighted. Like the man of Bethsaida, I need to look intently, carefully and to keep looking. I need to see Jesus for who He is and to keep Him in my sights. The Message version puts it this way. "The man looked hard and realized that he had recovered perfect sight, saw everything in bright, twenty-twenty focus". v 26

May we have Jesus in twenty-twenty focus and follow Him.

The Faith of the Centurion: Luke 7 v 1-10

There are things about me that you need to know. I am a Gentile, but a God fearer, and sympathetic to the Jewish faith and nation. I have many friends who are Jews and being of significant wealth, I helped to finance the building of the synagogue here in Capernaum. I am a centurion at the Capernaum Roman garrison being responsible for about a hundred Roman troops stationed here. I realize that to many, I represent enemy occupation, but I have tried to be humane and sensitive to a horrendous situation. I believe that I have secured the favour of the local people. I am a person in authority, but I am also a person under the authority and rule of others. I understand authority, leadership, and the chain of command. I understand the power of commands and orders and I can recognize such authority in others.

I have a loyal squad and value those who work for me and under me. Sadly, one of my special servants, someone I value highly, became seriously ill, to the point of death. I heard that a Jesus of Nazareth, a Jew, and His followers had just entered Capernaum. I had heard many things about this teacher and recognized His growing power and authority, even to heal. He seemed to be a person with the power of words, and authority over sickness. By reputation He was a godly man under the authority of God Himself. I was anxious that He should not feel concerned about a request from a Gentile Officer at an army garrison and so, I sent some Jewish elders, to speak on my behalf, with the request that He might come to heal my servant.

But as I considered our different positions in society- Gentile and Jew, Army Captain and charismatic teacher and healer, yet both with authority to issue a clear command and the word would be done, I then sent a few faithful friends to the Teacher with the following message. "Lord, I do not consider myself worthy to come to you myself, or for you to enter my house, so I simply ask that you just say the word, and my servant will be healed. Do not trouble yourself to come-just say the word."

A short while later, as I checked on my servant, to my delight and amazement, I discovered that he was well and was anxious to go about his duties once again. As my friends and the Jewish elders returned to my home, they reported their conversations with Jesus, the Teacher. Jesus had commended me, a gentile, a centurion, an enemy of the Jewish nation, for my faith in Him and because of my faith in Him, my servant was healed.

His friends had said to Jesus, "He is worthy." The centurion himself said, "I am not worthy." "I am-not worthy to come to you or for you to come to my house" but he recognized One who was worthy.

Then I looked, and I heard around the throne and the living creatures and the elders the voice of many angels, numbering myriads of myriads and thousands of thousands, saying with a loud voice, "Worthy is the Lamb who was slain, to receive power and wealth and wisdom and might and honour and glory and blessing!" Revelation 5 v 12

Jairus: Jesus is never too late

I am one of the rulers in the Capernaum synagogue, well known, a person of status, and position with responsibilities and power, but I am also a father, in anguish, consumed by grief, misery, distress and worry. My only child, my little girl of only twelve years, so desperately ill, is now seemingly at the point of death. I have heard that this Jesus, the Nazarene, the One that the Pharisees and religious groups say that we should shun, has been doing amazing things and has even healed some. So, what am I to do? I am desperate, my heart is breaking, I have exhausted all other means of help and I will do anything to save my child. It was, in the end, an easy thing to do. The Jesus Teacher was surrounded by the crowd. People were crushing in from all sides, pressing in, this mass of human need surrounding, encircling, enclosing Him and almost swallowing Him up. It was so clear as to who He was. There was no mistake. I pushed a path through the crowd, some moving to let me pass, recognizing me, others had no such manners and pressed in more closely, some even blocking my way, but I had to reach my only source of hope.

My colleagues would be shocked to know and hear of what I did next. But I had no concern now for my reputation or standing at the synagogue, my pride or position in the community. I approached and fell at His feet, pleading with Him to come with me to my house and to lay His hands on my little daughter. The situation was urgent, critical, time was of the essence, there could be no delay or attempt to find a new solution. As soon as His gaze turned to me, and He saw my need, my longing, I could sense His gentle strength and knew that He would respond. But now the crowd grew even larger, curious, moving in still closer to hear my words. Then, the unexpected interruption happened. He stopped abruptly, aware of another individual need in the crowd. A woman had reached out to Him for healing- another desperate, anguished soul. But please, oh please do not delay further, how long will this take, I cannot bear this delay, this setback that will hold up any chance of us getting to my daughter. But the Teacher was unhurried, calm, firmly but gently in control of all that was happening. He called the woman, 'daughter', commended her faith and trust in Him, confirmed her healing and invited her to go home in peace. He called her 'daughter'. It should have given me hope and reassurance, but I was more distressed and agitated. And then something traumatic happened. Some people from my house arrived with the crushing and devastating news. "Your daughter is dead. Do not trouble the teacher anymore." It was abrupt, stark, shocking. I nearly fell to my knees again. This was too much to bear. Had the Teacher come straight away could she have been saved?

My mind was reeling. I felt physical pain and grief. I had reached the end. But the Teacher spoke gently, lovingly and with no sense of hurry or urgency, simply said, "Do not be afraid, only believe and she will be healed." Three short phrases. I will remember those words for the rest of my life. As I think back to those words now, I think, for what or who or how was I supposed to believe? But I was asked to believe. His words meant that there is nothing to be afraid of. Be calm. Hold on to me for this. Count on me. Be assured. I had no energy to do anything else. From leading Him, I was now following Him to the door of my home.

We were met by such a commotion and din. People were wailing and crying. The sound of their lamenting was a dreadful painful sound to the ears and the heart. The wailing soon turned to derision and scorn as Jesus stated that the girl was only sleeping. But with calm authority he disbanded the family mourners and crowd and a small group of us entered the room to be faced with the bed on which my daughter was laid.

Jesus took her hand in His and with a word of gentleness and love, with life giving power and authority, He just said, "little girl, get up." And she did. It was as if she had just been asleep and was now woken by a loving voice. We were floored- quite literally! How can you go from desperate grief and loss to sudden elation and joy in a matter of seconds?

Her life was restored. My life was restored. How can I explain what has just happened? But Jesus told us to say nothing. I do not have the words to explain. Where would I begin?

Jesus was not delayed. He was not late. The time element did not matter to Him. He had plenty of time. It would all be done in His good time.

Thoughts

There are times when we are in distress, confused, struggling with a problem and we have prayed and yet our prayers have hit the ceiling. We long for God to intervene and yet there is delay, protracted delay and waiting. Nothing changes. But our time scale is not the same as His. In His wisdom, He will act when the time is right. Can we trust His timing? Can we be patient while we wait? In the Gospel accounts there were other individuals who felt that Jesus had come too late. But Jesus had a loving purpose.

Wait and see what He will do.

Then Martha said to Jesus, "Lord, if You had been here, my brother would not have died.

When Mary came [to the place] where Jesus was and saw Him, she fell at His feet, saying to Him, "Lord, if You had been here, my brother would not have died.

I waited patiently for the Lord; he inclined to me and heard my cry.
He drew me up from the desolate pit, out of the miry bog,
and set my feet upon a rock, making my steps secure.
He put a new song in my mouth, a song of praise to our God.
Many will see and fear, and put their trust in the Lord. Psalm 27

Let us then fearlessly and confidently and boldly draw near to the throne of grace (the throne of God's unmerited favour to us sinners), that we may receive mercy [for our failures] and find grace to help in good time for every need [appropriate help and well-timed help, coming just when we need it]. Hebrews 4 v 16

Wait for the Lord; be strong, and let your heart take courage; yea, wait for the Lord! Psalm 40

The Samaritan woman

Some years ago, I spent a short time in Herat, Afghanistan, teaching at an International School and I had to adopt certain important cultural sensitivities. As a woman, I had to dress with my head, hair, neck, wrist, and ankles always covered and in modest Afghan dress. I had to avert my eyes if men approached, I would never speak to a man in public and always I sat with and joined a group of women. Women would always sit with the women in a different room to the men. I had to walk in front of or behind the house security guard by a suitable distance when we were walking on the road. He did not wish to be seen with a westerner. This was how things were done.

The encounter between Jesus and the Samaritan woman is one that never should have taken place if normal protocols had been followed. The woman was avoiding any contact with others by collecting water at noon and Jewish men would have avoided any association with this foreign woman. She would have turned away and returned later avoiding even eye contact with the stranger. However, Jesus goes against all the rules and not only remains seated at the well but speaks to her and goes further by making a request of her.

Jesus created an opening, recognizing her deep needs. He opens a safe space for her. As Jesus asks His probing questions, He creates the potential for a new perspective. His approach is gentle. His questioning sensitive and insightful. He challenges her about her life choices, but He does not condemn or damage her self-esteem, so that later she can say "He told me everything that I've ever done." He sees that she is searching for a spiritual understanding and begins to help her focus. She knows that someone called Messiah is coming. Catching the depth of her understanding, searching, and longing, Jesus leads her forward and openly declares to her who He is.

Jesus is a model of empathy, insight, and compassion. His understanding and perception of her, deep and focussed. His own needs for food, rest and resourcing are laid aside. He is available to help to meet her needs. The conversation with Jesus gave the woman a testimony to share with others and leading from that, many people in the town came to believe in Him. "Many of the Samaritans from that town believed in him because of the woman's testimony."

In our conversations, we may be listening to someone who is sharing their story. We do not know the experience, trials, circumstances, and personal situations behind their mask. We need this same sensitivity and compassion.

But the Lord said to Samuel, The Lord does not look at the things people look at. People look at the outward appearance, but the Lord looks at the heart. 1 Samuel 16 v 7 NIV

Pray
For girls and women, in predominantly Muslim countries, where they are vulnerable, unable to play a role in their societies, and may often abused and persecuted. For places and circumstances where there is persecution of Christians and their communities. For those in our society who feel that they have no voice. As we speak with each other, may we hear the unspoken words and needs. May our testimony and words attract others and share your good news.

The voice of a bystander: John 8 v 1-11

It was Tabernacles, and such a fun time to be at the temple- a celebration of harvest and joy, thankfulness, promises, a time of remembering, sharing and family togetherness. Today was so special as there was a new young teacher and such a large crowd to hear Him. His ideas were so fresh, so gentle, so different and the claims that He was making-well, they would get Him into trouble! I could already see some harsh and angry faces among the temple leaders. But for most of us, the common people, we were curious. We were all whispering about Him, though we dared not speak out or be overheard. I heard some people say that He was a prophet or even the Messiah. Some whispered that they had seen Him perform a miracle. But we kept quiet out of fear of the Pharisees.

Then something alarming, horrifying, happened. Some teachers of the Law of Moses and a group of Pharisees brought in a woman and made her stand before everyone in the very centre of the Temple Court, right in front of the Teacher. The poor creature was dishevelled, frightened, humiliated and exposed to everyone's judgement and public display. They announced her crime to all present and demanded a judgement from the Teacher. Then the strangest of things happened. The angry mood quietened, the crowd became silent and expectant, and the Teacher, ignoring their questions, simply bent down to the ground and began to draw or write with his finger in the sand beneath His feet. I tried to push forward to see what the words might be. I tried to see what He was writing. How strange was this! The loaded questions from the Leaders kept coming, forcefully, angrily. But He was unperturbed, calm, with an air of quiet authority as He stood up and looking directly at them, invited those without sin to be the first to stone her. Then the strangeness continued as He bent down to the ground again and started to write. I hardly dare tell you what happened next. Without a word, the leaders and Pharisees began to skulk away and walk into the crowd. One by one they went. Not a word was said. That was some retreat! They had failed to get Jesus to fall into their trap. Everyone was in a stunned silence.

The poor woman was left alone, with her shame and condemnation, in front of the Teacher. Then the Teacher straightened up and looked at her - deep into her eyes. A simple question followed." Has no one condemned you?" In her trembling voice, she answered "no one, Sir." "Then neither do I condemn you but go and sin no more." She no longer had to fear those who were threatening her life. The Teacher was gentle, respectful. His words were words of grace as He gave her a new direction-, a turning point.

I'd give a month's wages to know what He wrote on the ground. Was He just gathering His thoughts? Was He silently speaking to His God? Was He writing the names of God - *The Lord our righteousness, the Lord who sanctifies, the Lord who heals?* We will never know.

The woman gathered her few tattered garments closely to her and walked out of the temple court. I never saw or heard of her again.

There is therefore now no condemnation for those who are in Christ Jesus. For the law of the Spirit of life in Christ Jesus has set me free from the law of sin and death. Romans 8 v 1-2

The Pharisees were using this woman as a tool, a non-person, an object lesson as they attempted to trap Jesus. Jesus saw her through eyes of love, and offered her grace, mercy and a turning point for her life.

Jesus, thou art all compassion, pure unbounded love thou art.
Visit us with thy salvation, enter every trembling heart.
Come, almighty to deliver, let us all thy grace receive.
Suddenly return, and never, never more thy temples leave.
Charles Wesley

A single touch

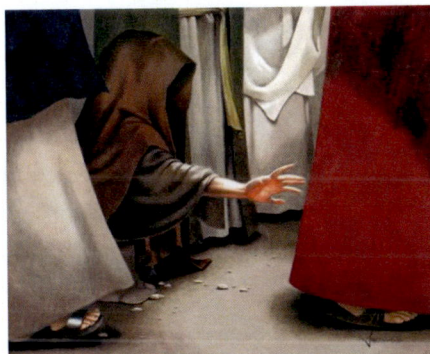

In Mark 5 v 24-34 we read the account of a woman who had suffered from a chronic illness for 12 years and who was hopeful of meeting Jesus secretly, but in plain sight.

She had endured years of misery, shame, isolation, and financial loss. The nature of her illness meant that she was treated as an outcast and unclean. She was fearful of any social interaction and so would have no independence or ability to move out of her home freely She was truly in a state of permanent lockdown. Her medical appointments and treatments meant that both her energy and money ebbed away, yet there was no relief or improvement- in fact her condition became worse. She was despairing, defeated and despondent. She was a prisoner to her illness with little prospect of hope or healing. And then she heard of Jesus. She may have heard Jairus's request to heal his twelve-year-old, daughter. If Jesus was willing to go with this desperate father, then surely there was hope for his child and now also for her. She dared to believe. "If I just touch His clothing, I will be healed". She was determined to go to Jesus for healing. But she could not do this openly. By this time, a huge crowd had gathered around Jesus pressing in from every side. She came in fear and trembling, hiding her identity. She could not risk being seen and so she came behind him secretly, slipping in under the cover of the jostling crowd and reached out to touch his outer robe. She dared to believe that this one single touch would bring her the healing that she was so desperate for.

As soon as she touched the cloth, she knew that she had been healed. There was no doubt in her mind and in her body. How could she control the emotions and thoughts suddenly flooding through her mind? And now she hoped to steal away quietly. She had come secretly but she could not leave secretly. His voice rang out asking "Who touched me?" His searching gaze swept across the crowds looking at the faces of those around him to see who had done this. Would she dare to identify herself? In great fear, perhaps more of the crowd than her Healer, she raised her head and returned to fall at his feet, once again in fear and trembling and recounted her story-the whole crowd listening to her account.

Jesus desired her to go in peace, not with fear, secrecy, and uncertainty. His purpose was one of love for her. The whole crowd would see and hear her. They would hear Jesus call her "daughter". They would hear Jesus commend her faith "your faith has healed you". and His blessing to "go in peace". No longer would she need to hide away like the leper that she once felt that she was. She was free of shame and sickness and free to hold her head up in the crowd. "Be freed from your suffering". She would now be free in so many ways.

Praise the Lord for it is good to sing praise to our God.
For He is gracious, and a song of praise is seemly.
The Lord builds up Jerusalem, He gathers the outcasts of Israel.
He heals the broken hearted and binds up their wounds.
Psalm 147 v 2

PRAY

I bind unto myself today the power of God to hold and lead.
His eye to watch, His might to stay. His ear to hearken to my need.
The wisdom of my God to teach. His hand to guide, His shield to ward.
The word of God to give me speech, His heavenly host to be my guard.
From the Hymn of St Patrick

Songs at Midnight Paul and Silas

Let me introduce myself. I live in Philippi, a Roman outpost, and a major city in Macedonia. It is normally a trouble-free town, as far as major incidents are concerned, but on this one day, and this one night, the most amazing things took place. I am the senior gaoler at the Philippi prison under Roman authority. But let me begin at the beginning.

In the town, there is a female slave with a spirit of divination by which she can predict the future. She has earned a lucrative amount of money for her slave owners by her fortune-telling, and they were a very familiar sight around the marketplace and the river. Everyone knew her-and the slave owners. Two men had newly arrived in the town, visitors, and they had spent time around the place of prayer near the river and in the marketplace. This woman had taken to following them around each day, pestering them and shouting out, "These men are working for the most high God. They're laying out the road of salvation for you!" She did this for several days until the two men and her slave owners began to be annoyed and frustrated by her behaviour.

One of the men, finally fed up with her, turned and commanded the spirit that possessed her, to come out of her. And it was gone, just like that. Now, this did not please her slave owners who realized that their lucrative business, and money, had come to an end.

The slave dragged the two men to the marketplace where a crowd, or rather a mob, quickly gathered. They called out, "These men are Jews and are throwing our city into an uproar by advocating customs unlawful for us Romans to accept or practice," they declared. So, fearful of a riot, the Magistrates ordered the men to be stripped, beaten with rods, publicly flogged, and then thrown into prison. I was given special orders to guard them carefully and so I put them into the inner, deepest cell, the maximum-security area, in the deepest hole of the prison, with their feet fastened in the stocks, and locked with chains.

Now, I have never met men like these two men, and I am used to prisoners and roughnecks. But these men were quite different. But let me go on with my story. From the deepest hole of the prison, we heard singing, and hymns of praise and prayers to God. I have never heard anything like it! And all the prisoners were listening to their songs of praise and worship. Then at midnight, I guess, a violent earthquake occurred, shaking and breaking up the very foundations of the prison. The prison doors were flung open, the doors hung on their hinges, and the prisoners' chains were released. I was fearing for my own life too. All the prisoners could have escaped, with the two new prisoners. I called for lights, rushed in, and trembling all over, fell at the feet of the two men still sitting where I had first placed them. They looked untroubled, calm, as they wriggled out of the chains and stocks, covered in dust, brick, and bits of wood.

Then they looked at me with such kindness and spoke gently to me. Despite my fears for my job, my life, and my Roman overlords, I took them to my house and offered them food. Then, they began to talk to me about a man called Jesus, a Saviour. It was late into the night, the middle of the night, but I took them outside and washed their wounds. Then I said, "Sirs, what must I do to be saved?" And they replied, "Believe in the Lord Jesus and then you will be saved, you and your household." We overjoyed at finding faith in God, and we were all baptised without delay.

Now here is the thing. These men had endured abuse, hostility, prejudice, beatings, flogging and the maximum-security 'hole in the ground' prison. But still, they could pray, sing, and praise their God. Where there could have been groans, cries of pain and misery, complaints of unjust treatment and abuse, there were songs of joy and praise.

Advent

Disruption

Having a child brings a major change and disruption to your normal way of living. There is no going back! Whether a pregnancy is planned, longed for or unexpected, the changes that come with a new child cause major upheaval, changes of lifestyle, an interruption to normal ways of working and daily routines, and can often bring confusion, doubts, and concerns- along with great joys. As new parents Phil and I often felt that we should have badges made with the slogan- "I'm sorry, I haven't a clue" as we dealt with each new challenge.

For two central and significant people in the Christmas accounts, Elizabeth and Mary, there would be a significant disruption to their existing way of life, and their view of themselves. The changes announced by Gabriel would be sudden, all encompassing, and radical, affecting their lives, circumstances, and relationships. This major disruption, this sudden change to their normal way of life and function, would create a disturbance, an upheaval, and an interruption to how they viewed their lives and their futures. These changes would no doubt cause confusion as they faced the unexpected and the new.

Elizabeth was far advanced in years, childless and barren but was known as a righteous woman, a descendant of the priestly line of Aaron who walked blamelessly before God. Elizabeth would bear a child in her old age to Zachariah. We read that for five months she secluded herself away.

Sometime later Elizabeth knew she was to become a mother. She kept herself hidden for five months. She said, "This is what the Lord has done for me. He has looked on me and has taken away my shame from among men." Luke 1 v 24-25 NLV

Mary was a young woman, from the small town of Nazareth in Galilee. She was a virgin promised in marriage to Joseph, of the family and line of David. The Angel tells Mary that she has found favour with God and uniquely chosen to bear the Son of God. Receiving this news, Mary was greatly troubled, disturbed and confused, with a multitude of thoughts spinning around in her mind. Mary's" yes" meant that she was accepting a life changing role with its many consequences. The way ahead was unknown. Joseph, her family, and her community could reject her. How could she possibly explain what was to happen to her? Yet, her acceptance placed her in the will of her God.

"See, your cousin Elizabeth, as old as she is, is going to give birth to a child. She was not able to have children before, but now she is in her sixth month. For God can do all things." Then Mary said, "I am willing to be used of the Lord. Let it happen to me as you have said." Then the angel went away from her. Luke 1 v 37-38 NLV

I love the fact that Mary and Elizabeth spent three months together at Elizabeth's home prior to the birth of John. This would be a time of great comfort, sharing and privacy. How could you share these deeply personal matters more widely? So, their shared experience would lead to a deeper understanding.

We often face times of great disruption and turbulence. There may be a sudden change of direction or circumstance. But God will be there- and there may also be a kindred spirit who knows what you are going through.

A Prayer Father, sometimes life is hard, and I kick against the demands and the course of my life. I would like things to be easy, comfortable, convenient, and straightforward, knowing the direction and purpose of the path in front of me. Sometimes there is an unexpected turn in the road which causes disruption, a disturbance, or a change of direction. Life is uncertain, unpredictable, difficult and I often fail to see the way in front of me. But you have promised a light for my path. Help me to trust you one step at a time, not with resignation but with gladness and trust that you know the end from the beginning. Your purpose for me is true and good.

A Blessing for After

This blessing
is for the moment
after clarity has come,
after inspiration,
after you have agreed
to what seems
impossible.

This blessing
is what follows
after illumination departs
and you realize
there is no map
for the path
you have chosen,
no one to serve
as guide,
nothing to do
but gather up
your gumption
and set out.

This blessing
will go with you.
It carries no answers,

no charts,
no plans.

It carries no source
of light
within itself.

But in its pocket
is tucked a mirror
that, from time to time,
it will hold up to you.

to remind you
of the radiance
that came
when you gave
your awful and wondrous
yes.

Jan Richardson

Waiting

Waiting can be hard, long, and frustrating. I could not begin to add up the number of hours that I have spent in my adult lifetime to date, waiting- waiting for the birth of a child; waiting at the doctors, clinic or hospital; waiting at the school gate, activity club, church hall; waiting for the production or concert to begin; waiting for the children's exam results, decisions after interviews; waiting for the much needed holiday, or for long expected news. Waiting involves the expectation or hope that something will happen, being in readiness for its beginning or coming, and waiting with patience during the indeterminate period before the arrival or completion of the expected hope. I am well practised at waiting. But for many people, waiting is hard.

In the accounts of the birth of Jesus, there is a lot of waiting by a lot of people- Zechariah and Elizabeth, Mary, and the elderly prophets at the Temple gate, Simeon, and Anna. For these people, their waiting was longed for, prayed for, and anticipated.

Zechariah and Elizabeth had prayed for and longed for a child. In their old age, Gabriel was sent to them with the news of the birth of their child, John. 'But the angel said to him: "Do not be afraid, Zechariah; your prayer has been heard. Your wife Elizabeth will bear you a son, and you are to call him John.' Luke 1 v 13

Gabriel was also sent to the young Mary with news of the promised Saviour that she would bear. Mary's pregnancy and waiting could have been a troubling and anxious time as she no doubt faced the questions and quizzical looks of neighbours and villagers. But she would take comfort in the company of her cousin Elizabeth as they waited together. Mary would later endure a journey to Bethlehem, an anxious search for a safe place to deliver her baby, followed by a hurried escape to Egypt. There, Joseph, Mary and Jesus would be strangers and refugees for two years until they were able to return to their hometown. Waiting. Waiting for the right time. The safe time.

Simeon, a righteous and devout man, living in Jerusalem, 'was eagerly waiting for the Messiah to come and rescue Israel. The Holy Spirit was upon him and had revealed to him that he would not die until he had seen the Lord's Messiah.' Luke 2 v 25-26 Simeon was led to the Temple by the Holy Spirit, at the exact time that Joseph and Mary arrived with the eight-day old infant, Jesus, at the Temple for the ceremony of purification and circumcision. Simeon's long wait was at an end.

Anna, an 84-year-old, widow, and prophet who worshipped daily at the Temple in Jerusalem, was also waiting, as were other worshippers, hoping for God's intervention in Israel. 'She never left the temple but worshiped night and day, fasting and praying. Coming up to them at that very moment, she gave thanks to God and spoke about the child to all who were looking forward to the redemption of Jerusalem'. Luke 2 v 37-38

From infant to child to man, John and Jesus waited until the time was right for them to begin their appearances and ministries on the world's stage. We believe that Jesus was about thirty years old before He began His ministry. 'Jesus came into Galilee, proclaiming the Gospel of God, saying, "The time has come at last—the kingdom of God has arrived. You must change your hearts and minds and believe the good news." Mark 1 v 15

Waiting and perfect timing. The time had come at last. God's timing is always precise, and perfect. He steps in at the right time-the 'Kairos' time-"the appointed time in the purposes of God."

Song
Strength will rise as we wait upon the Lord
We will wait upon the Lord, we will wait upon the Lord
Strength will rise as we wait upon the Lord
We will wait upon the Lord, we will wait upon the Lord.
Our God, you reign forever
Our hope, our strong Deliverer.
Chris Tomlin

Hymn
Come, Thou long expected Jesus
Born to set Thy people free;
From our fears and sins release us,
Let us find our rest in Thee.

Charles Wesley

PRAY. For those who are waiting-for news, for appointments, for surgery, for an answer to a longing prayer. Help us to trust God's perfect timing in our waiting.

Perfect Timing

(Ecclesiastes 3.11)

"He has made everything beautiful in its time. He has also set eternity in the human heart; yet no one can fathom what God has done from beginning to end."

BIBLE
INSPIRE.COM

Have you ever felt that you have just walked into the right place at the right time and met the right people? The timing feels to be perfect and precise, as if it was always meant to be.

In the narrative of the birth of Jesus in Luke 2 I was challenged by the two elderly prophets, Simeon and Anna. Clearly, their arrival on the scene, just as the family arrived for Jesus's dedication in the Temple at Jerusalem, was no happenstance. It was no coincidence or just good timing, because they were frequent attenders to the Temple Court. No. These two faithful worshippers were directed by the Holy Spirit to that very point, on that very day, at that very time, when Mary, Joseph and the infant Jesus arrived in the Temple Court.

The Holy Spirit was upon Simeon and prompted by the Holy Spirit he came into the Temple enclosure at the perfectly planned, precise time. *'Prompted by the Spirit, Simeon came into the Temple enclosure; and when the parents brought in the child Jesus, to do for Him the custom required by the Law, Simeon took Him into his arms, and blessed, praised, and thanked God'. Luke 2 v 27-28 AMP.* Prompted by the Holy Spirit, Simeon spoke prophetic words over the child, calling Jesus a Light for the revelation of the Gentiles, and God's salvation. Simeon then addressed Mary with prophetic words. Simeon had been promised, again by the Holy Spirit, that he would not see death until he had seen the Lord's Messiah. Simeon's arrival, actions, and words at this point, were all directed by the Holy Spirit. He had waited many years for this precise moment in time.

Anna spent her days at the Temple serving and worshiping night and day, with fasting and prayers. But, at the precise time that Simeon was speaking with Joseph and Mary, she came along to that very spot, at that very time to the Temple enclosure. 'She came along just as Simeon was talking with Mary and Joseph, and she also began thanking God and telling everyone in Jerusalem who had been awaiting the coming of the Savior that the Messiah had finally arrived'. Luke 2 v 38 TLB

The Message version says, 'At the very time Simeon was praying, she showed up, broke into an anthem of praise to God, and talked about the child to all who were waiting expectantly for the freeing of Jerusalem.' Anna sang an anthem of praise to God. Anna had waited patiently for many years for this precise moment in time.

Simeon and Anna were two faithful worshippers, filled with the Holy Spirit, waiting for the arrival of Messiah. The Holy Spirit prompted their attendance at the Temple when the timing was perfect. They had listened to the promptings of the Holy Spirit.

The Holy Spirit will prompt us too, with His peace, and His Presence. We need to be patient as we wait for God's perfect time. God is never in a hurry and though the waiting is hard we should not rush on ahead. There may be something that we have longed for, prayed for and we have become impatient and even discontented. But trust His timing. He knows the perfect time.

From long ago no ear has heard and no eye has seen any God besides You, who works for those who wait for Him. You meet him who finds joy in doing what is right and good, who remembers You in Your ways. Isaiah 64 v 4-5 NLV

He has made everything beautiful in its time. Ecclesiastes 3 v 11

PRAY for God's perfect timing and for patience in the waiting.

Treasure

I have many treasure boxes, safely stored away, containing artefacts, documents, certificates, photographs, albums, and a whole range of objects, large and small, and these treasure troves contain precious memories of children, parents, grandparents, and wider family members. I have an archive of family records and documents which have become records of our ancestry, and which are an important store of memories. After the deaths of his parents, we helped Sam to collect memory boxes of the important objects, letters, photos, cards, items of clothing, and personal items that had belonged to Richard and Charlotte and which would become his precious memories and his personal treasure store. This kind of treasure is vital and life giving.

Mary had her own personal treasure store- a store of precious words and statements about her child, Jesus, which would always remain with her.

But Mary treasured up all these things and pondered them in her heart. Luke 2 v 19

Mary kept all these things to herself, holding them dear, deep within herself. Luke 2 v 19 MSG

There were many things that Mary was told about her new baby Son.

The Angel announced that *"The Holy Spirit will come upon you, and the power of the Most High will overshadow you. So, the baby to be born will be holy, and he will be called the Son of God. He will be very great and will be called the Son of the Most High. The Lord God will give him the throne of his ancestor David. And he will reign over Israel forever; his Kingdom will never end. Luke 1 v 32-35 NLT*

From Joseph she was told that her Son was Holy Spirit conceived and that He was to be called "Jesus— 'God saves'—because He will save His people from their sins."

From the shepherds she learned: that His birth was a joyful event, meant for everyone, worldwide. That He was Saviour, Messiah, and Master.

From Simeon, Mary learned that He was salvation in person, a God revealing light to the non-Jewish nations and the glory of God's people Israel, a sign from God Himself, and a 'heart revealer.'

Mary would hear from the Maji, the title, the King of the Jews and the words of Micah referring to the Messiah. These great men, scholars who had searched records, documents, scriptures, and prophecies, had followed a guiding star to worship her child and would kneel in worship opening their luggage and presenting gifts of gold, frankincense, myrrh.

So, Mary privately treasured all these words. These words were her treasure store, her memory box of wonderful, precious things. She stored them away in her heart and mind as she watched her Son, Jesus grow into manhood.

We have treasure that we can store in our hearts. This treasure is the knowledge of Jesus, God's Son, Emmanuel, the Wonderful Counsellor, the Prince of Peace who has come to bring salvation.

I want you woven into a tapestry of love, in touch with everything there is to know of God. Then you will have minds confident and at rest, focused on Christ, God's great mystery. All the richest treasures of wisdom and knowledge are embedded in that mystery and nowhere else. And we've been shown the mystery! Colossians 2 v 3 MSG

But this precious treasure—this light and power that now shine within us— is held in a perishable container, that is, in our weak bodies. Everyone can see that the glorious power within must be from God and is not our own. 2 Corinthians 4 v 7 TLB

Open Arms

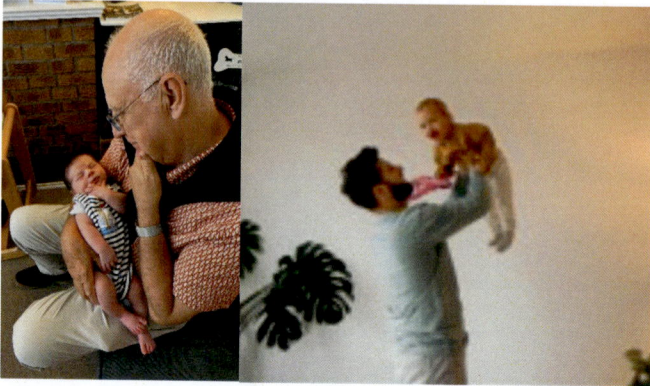

When any of our family come to visit us, we normally rush from the house to the driveway to 'welcome them with open arms.' The grandchildren are often welcomed with a wide hug or picked up with a swirl around in the air-depending on their size of course. When each of the newborns arrived, we made sure that we visited, either hospital or home, and welcomed each one into our arms with great joy. It is a delight to welcome a new baby into the family.

For Simeon, his welcoming of the eight-day old infant Jesus, was a very significant event. It had been revealed to Simeon by the Holy Spirit that he would not see death until he had seen with his own eyes the Lord's Messiah. 'Led by the Spirit, Simeon went into the Temple. When the parents brought the child Jesus into the Temple to do for him what the Law required, Simeon took the child in his arms and gave thanks to God.' Luke 2 v 27-28

Simeon took the eight-day old baby into his arms, holding him with arms of love and welcome, and again by the Holy Spirit spoke powerful prophetic words, and words of blessing, over the child and Mary, His mother. Simeon praised His God and blessed the young family. *"Lord,"* he said, *"now I can die content! For I have seen Him as you promised me I would. I have seen the Saviour you have given to the world. He is the Light that will shine upon the nations, and He will be the glory of your people Israel!" Joseph and Mary just stood there, marvelling at what was being said about Jesus. Luke 2 v 29-33*

For many individuals and families, 2024 has been a challenging year, but as we look forward to a new year, with whatever it may hold for us, we can be assured that God is faithful and that He holds us securely. He is our refuge, and He does not just hold us in His arms, but He carries us close to His heart.

The eternal God is your refuge, and underneath are the everlasting arms. Deuteronomy 33 v 27

He tends his flock like a shepherd:
*   He gathers the lambs in his arms*
and carries them close to his heart;
*   He gently leads those that have young. Isaiah 40 v 10-11*

Then Jesus placed a little child among them; and taking the child in his arms He said to them, "Anyone who welcomes a little child like this in my name is welcoming me, and anyone who welcomes me is welcoming my Father who sent me!" Mark 9 v 36-37

And Jesus took the children in his arms, placed his hands on them and blessed them. Mark 10 v 16

So, he got up and went to his father.   "But while he was still a long way off, his father saw him and was filled with compassion for him; he ran to his son, threw his arms around him and kissed him. Luke 15 v 20

A Blessing:

Bless all who worship You, from the rising of the sun unto the going down of the same. Of Your goodness, give us; with Your love, inspire us, by Your spirit guide us; by Your power, protect us; in Your mercy receive us now and always. AMEN

(An Ancient Collect)

Steps into the new year

As we take our first, few steps into this new year, we cannot know what 2025 will hold for us. There may be unexpected joys or trials, new challenges begun, or opportunities missed, dreams realized, or ambitions and hopes lost, new friendships begun, or familiar traditions lost. It may be a blessing and a grace that we cannot know the details as the year unfolds before us. We are asked only to step forward in faith, one step at a time.

I am reminded of the accounts of the Maji, who stepped out on their long and uncertain journey, to find the promised child. The routes and resting places of their journey would be unfamiliar, hazardous at times, and strange. Their journey, with its distances, cost, risks, and the uncertainty of success, was perhaps their daily reality and challenge. There would be moments of confusion, as at Herod's palace, when they failed to find the expected One, although the star was still present. But despite the hardships, the unexpected, and the uncertainties, they kept travelling towards the child.

So, as we go into this new year, may we be guided by wisdom, courage, compassion, and the light of the Christ child. Let us cherish the joys, learn from the trials, and remain open to the countless possibilities that await us. May we take each step with intention and grace, and may our journey be filled with love, grace, growth, and new possibilities.

"The road is revealed by turns you could not have foreseen." Jan Richardson

A Prayer for the Year ahead:

I arise today
Through a mighty strength:
God's power to guide me,
God's might to uphold me,
God's eyes to watch over me;
God's ear to hear me,
God's word to give me speech,
God's hand to guard me,
God's way to lie before me,
God's shield to shelter me,
God's host to secure me.

(First Millennium - Bridgid of Gael)

Stop, Stay, Go

The Maji followed God's leading by signs, star, and dream. They had ignored the disquieting voices in their heads and around them, that may have told them that they were unwise to take such a journey. But their instincts, the quiet prompting of God, and their research, told them to follow the rising, leading star. After finding the infant, and in response to a dream, they were guided to find a new way home, avoiding a return to Herod's palace. This new journey would be without the comfort of the leading star but God, in His mercy, gave His protection and safety to the

Maji. They trusted and followed the dream's instruction and the guidance of God.

They returned to their own country by another route because God had warned them in a dream not to go back to Herod. Matthew 2 v 12

Protection, safety, and guidance had been given to Joseph, Mary, and the child Jesus. Joseph, being warned by an angel of the Lord in a dream to escape from Herod and his anger, escaped with his   family to Egypt, leaving hurriedly, in the middle of the night. They remained there as strangers, and refugees in a foreign land, because Herod's clear intention was to search for and destroy the child. *"Stay there until you hear from Me." Matthew 2 v 13*

I love that phrase 'stay there until you hear from me.' Joseph was told by God to wait for the right time and His guidance, which would allow the family to return to their homeland. He was to stay, to remain, to be settled, even though he could not know God's timing.

Two years later, and once again instructed in a dream, Joseph, Mary, and Jesus, returned to their homeland of Israel. With Joseph's wisdom and discernment, and God's clear direction, Joseph took his young family, to Nazareth, in the region of Galilee. Herod Archelaus was now ruling in place of his father Herod the Great, so Jesus could still be in danger. The Nazarenes were often treated with suspicion and caution by other Jews and Jesus was once called 'Jesus the Nazarene' in an insulting, derogatory way. But this move would perhaps keep Jesus safe. *'So, the family went and lived in a town called Nazareth. This fulfilled what the prophets had said: "He will be called a Nazarene."* Matthew 2 v22-23 NLT

Care, certainty, God's safe keeping and guidance are for those who trust in the name of the Lord. We may not have dreams, or hear angel voices, but we can lean into Him daily to know his presence with us and to find His direction. May we try not to look back, only forward to a new way, a new path, a new road. Not a star, but Jesus as the light for that new path, and this coming year. The Lord says, "I will guide you along the best pathway for your life. I will advise you and watch over you. Psalm 32 v 8 NLT

SONG: My Guardian

King of love and grace, my Guardian,
All my hopes and fears are in Your hands;
I'm in Your hands.
Where You go, I'll go; show me the way.
Every step I take be now my guide,
God on my side.
You go before me, You're there beside me,
And if I wander Love will find me.
Goodness and mercy will always follow.
You go before me, my Guardian.

Songwriters: Stuart Garrard / Ben Cantelon / Nick Herbert

Guardian lyrics © Stugio Music Publishing, Sony/atv Timber Publishing, Thankyou Music, Thank You Music Ltd.

Planting Peace

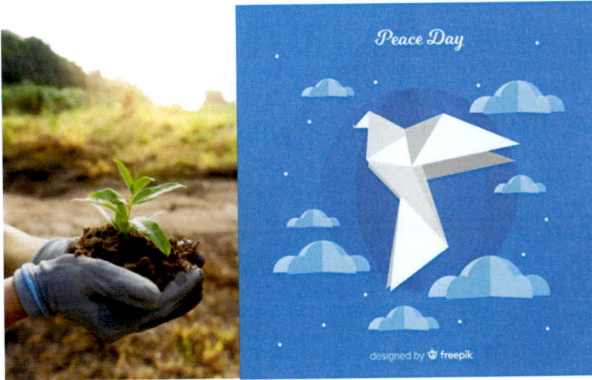

I am very poor at growing anything green. It might be seeds, houseplants, plants for the garden or vegetables. I can succeed with cress and hardy perennials such as lavender, but little else. My father was a member of a horticultural society, and we had a garden and a large allotment which we looked after every weekend, but I am afraid that I did not absorb his many gardening skills. But I am encouraged to be a planter of peace. Our world is a very troubled place and, in 2024 on our screens we have witnessed wars, disasters, heartaches, mental health crises in our young people and much more. So, as we enter a new year, may we endeavour to be planters of peace, whether we feel capable, skilled or woefully inadequate. May we offer love, joy, gentleness, along with peace, as we connect with others in our everyday. Help us to share the peace of the Prince of Peace.

A Prayer for Planting Peace:
(In the style of the prayer of St Francis of Assisi)
By Lizzie Ojo Martens

Lord as I reflect on the challenges present within my community
As well as my own lived experience,
I ask that you make me an instrument of your peace.
Where there is division, let me sow unity.
Where there is stigma, belonging.
Where there is unfamiliarity, awareness.
Where there is sorrow, joy.
Where there is silence or shame, light.
Where there is isolation, inclusion and companionship.
Where there is hopelessness, hope.
O Divine Counsellor, grant that I may not so much seek to be comforted,
but to comfort others
And to speak, as to listen.
For it is in giving that we receive,
And it is in your presence that we find peace.

For a child is born to us,
  a son is given to us.
The government will rest on his shoulders.
  And he will be called:
Wonderful Counsellor, Mighty God,
  Everlasting Father, Prince of Peace.
His government and its peace
  will never end.   *Isaiah 9 v 6-7 NLT*

In John 14 v 27 Jesus offers His shalom' peace. He 'bequeaths' His peace. Just as a rich person would bequeath property or something valuable to someone else, the peace of Jesus is bequeathed to us Jesus offers wholeness, completeness, soundness of spirit, soul and body, and wellbeing. This is His gift to us. Let us share this gift.

SONG

Let there be peace on earth
And let it begin with me
Let there be peace on Earth
The peace that was meant to be

Let peace begin with me
Let this be the moment now.

With every step I take
Let this be my solemn vow
To take each moment and live
Each moment in peace eternally
Let there be peace on earth
And let it begin with me

Songwriters: Jill Jackson & Sy Miller

Let There Be Peace on Earth lyrics © Music Copyright Consultant Grp

Prayers

Children learn what they live

If children live with criticism, they learn to condemn.

If children live with hostility, they learn to fight.

If children live with fear, they learn to be apprehensive.

If children live with pity, they learn to feel sorry for themselves.

If children live with ridicule, they learn to feel shy.

If children live with jealousy, they learn to feel envy.

If children live with shame, they learn to feel guilty.

If children live with encouragement, they learn confidence.

If children live with tolerance, they learn patience.

If children live with praise, they learn appreciation.

If children live with acceptance, they learn to love.

If children live with approval, they learn to like themselves.

If children live with recognition, they learn it is good to have a goal.

If children live with sharing, they learn generosity.

If children live with honesty, they learn truthfulness.

If children live with fairness, they learn justice.

If children live with kindness and consideration, they learn respect.

If children live with security, they learn to have faith in themselves and in those about them.

If children live with friendliness, they learn the world is a nice place in which to live.

Disturb us Lord

(Attributed to Sir Francis Drake)

Disturb us Lord, when we are too well pleased with ourselves.

when our dreams have come true, because we have dreamed too little.

when we arrive safely, because we sailed too close to the shore.

Disturb us Lord, when, with the abundance of things we possess, we have lost our thirst for the waters of life.

Having fallen in love with life, we have ceased to dream of eternity.

In our efforts to build a new earth, we have allowed our vision of the new Heaven to dim.

Disturb us Lord, to dare more boldly, to venture on wider seas, where storms will show your mastery.

Where, losing sight of land, we shall find the stars.

We ask you to push back the horizons of our hopes, as we sail into the future in strength, courage and love. Amen

Early Christian Prayers

I love early Christian prayers. They seem to provide a continuous link of worship between the early Christians of the first few centuries after the Crucifixion of Jesus and the struggles of the early church, to us today Their content and pattern can sometimes provide a useful template for the writing of modern prayers:

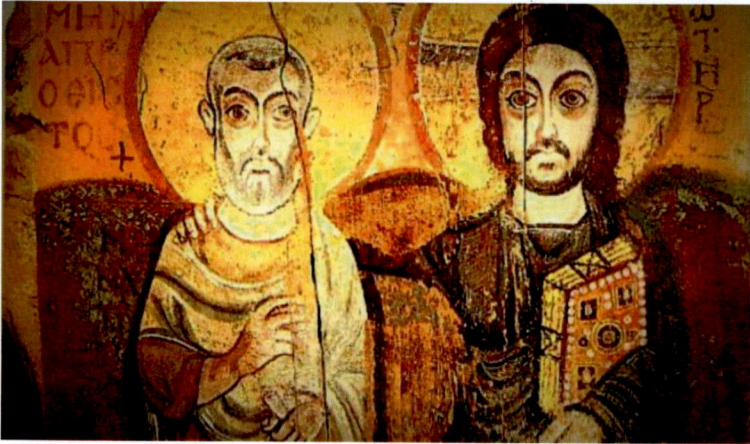

Look upon us, O Lord,
and let all the darkness of our souls
vanish before the beams of thy brightness.
Fill us with holy love,
and open to us the treasures of thy wisdom.
All our desire is known unto thee,
therefore perfect what thou hast begun,
and what thy Spirit has awakened us to ask in prayer.
We seek thy face,
turn thy face unto us and show us thy glory.
Then shall our longing be satisfied,
and our peace shall be perfect.
Augustine, 354 – 430

Thou Hast made us for Thyself, O Lord, and our hearts are restless until
they find their rest in Thee.
Augustine 354 - 430

O good shepherd, seek me out, and bring me home to thy fold again.
Deal favourably with me according to thy good pleasure,
till I may dwell in Thy house all the days of my life,
and praise Thee for ever and ever with them that are there.
Jerome, c 342 - 420

Lord, thou hast given us thy Word for a light to shine upon our path;
grant us so to meditate on that Word, and to follow its teaching,
that we may find in it the light that shines more and more until the
perfect day;
through Jesus Christ our Lord.
Jerome, c 342 – 420

O Lord, who hast mercy upon all, take away from me my sins,
and mercifully kindle in me the fire of thy Holy Spirit.
Take away from me the heart of stone,
and give me a heart of flesh,
a heart to love and adore thee,
a heart to delight in thee,
to follow and to enjoy thee,
for Christ's sake.
Ambrose of Milan, c 339-397

Alone with none but thee, my God,
I journey on my way.
What need I fear, when thou art near O king of night and day?
More safe am I within thy hand
Than if a host did round me stand.
Columba, c.521 - 597)

May God the Father bless us;
may Christ take care of us;
the Holy Ghost enlighten us all the days of our life.
The Lord be our defender and keeper of body and soul,
both now and for ever, to the ages of ages.
Æthelwold c 908-984

Lord, be with us this day,
Within us to purify us;
Above us to draw us up;
Beneath us to sustain us;
Before us to lead us;
Behind us to restrain us;
Around us to protect us.
Patrick c 389-461

O Sovereign and almighty Lord, bless all thy people, and all thy flock.
Give thy peace, thy help, thy love unto us thy servants, the sheep of thy
fold, that we may be united in the bond of peace and love, one body
and one spirit, in one hope of our calling, in thy divine and boundless
love.
Liturgy of St Mark, 2nd century

Teach us good Lord, to serve Thee as thou deservest.
To give and not to count the cost.
To fight and not to heed the wounds.
To toil and not to seek for rest.
To labour and not to ask for any reward, save that of knowing that we do
Thy will.
Ignatius of Loyola

Deep peace of the running wave to you.
Deep peace of the flowing air to you,
Deep peace of the quiet earth to you,
Deep peace of the shining stars to you,
Deep peace of the Son of Peace to you, for ever.
Source unknown - early Scottish

I rise today
Through the strength of heaven -
Light of sun,
Radiance of moon,
Splendour of fire,
Speed of lightning,
Swiftness of wind,
Depth of sea,
Stability of earth,
Firmness of rock.
Source unknown, early Scottish

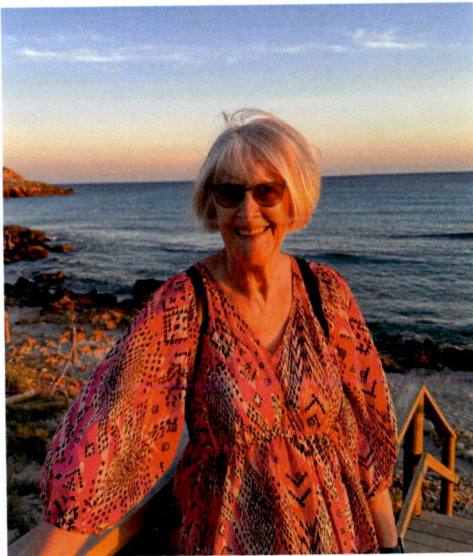